MW01030612

Michael McIntosh

SHOTGUNS AND SHOOTING

Michael McIntosh

SHOTGUNS AND SHOOTING

Illustrations by Eldridge Hardie
Foreword by Gene Hill

Countrysport Press
New Albany, Ohio

This edition of *Shotguns and Shooting* was printed by Jostens Book Manufacturing, State College, Pennsylvania. The book was designed by Saxon Design, Traverse City, Michigan. It is set in Bembo, which is modeled on typefaces cut by Francesco Griffo in 1495. It is considered one of the first of the oldstyle typefaces that were used as staple text types in Europe for 200 years. The special limited edition of this book is bound in Cabra leather and available in a signed and numbered edition of 250 copies.

10 9 8 7 6 5 4 3 2

Published by Countrysport Press
15 South High Street, New Albany, Ohio 43054-0166

Printed in the United States of America

Library of Congress Catalog Card Number: 95-067795
ISBN 0-924357-48-7 Trade Edition
ISBN 0-924357-49-5 Limited Edition

To Charles McIntosh
November 17, 1908–March 13, 1987
I wish you were here to read this, Dad,
because you started it all.

Contents

Part II:
Shooting—Craft, Cartridges, and Controversies

Craft

Cartridges

Controversies

Foreword

It's been quite a while since I wrote something with as much pure pleasure as this foreword. I feel like I'm introducing you to one of my favorite people—one I'm positive you'll like as much as I do.

I've listened often to Mike talk about guns, his delight and depth of knowledge polished pleasantly by a prose style that I envy as much as his insights and tidbits of lore. Here is a "best" writer revealing about all there is to know about "best" guns.

I'm not going to quote any of my favorite phrases; I'll let you have the delight of finding them yourself. They add a graceful note just when you'd love one and often remind me, rightly, of a critic detailing a work of art he's especially fond of.

Under this polished surface lies a work as carefully and thoroughly done as any on shotguns I've ever read—and with little modesty there are very few I haven't read. I'm often asked, "If you owned just one gun what would it be?" And I admit to waffling on my answer. But if you asked me if I could own only one book on shotguns, this would certainly be it.

As you'll see, Mike writes lovingly about the small things that contribute so much to the large—the pride in the hidden signature of a lockmaker, the fittings as measured by the thinness of smoke, and the tiny flourishes graven in the head of a screw. So it is in writing about something you care deeply about in both head and heart. Mike has engraved and polished the places most writers won't—or can't.

I add, only because there's no hint of it here, that Mike is a most accomplished shot; it's nice to know (and it's rare) that he can use a shotgun as handsomely as he writes about one.

That's enough from me. I want you to meet my friend Michael McIntosh. I know you'll get along famously.

Gene Hill
Oracle, Arizona

Preface

This book begins and ends with the presence of my father. This is appropriate, for my love of shotguns and shooting began with him, and probably will end there, too, somehow.

I've taken that love further than Dad had the opportunity to do, and guns have taken me farther in return. My one regret is that he isn't able to be with me, to share the shooting in the exotic places I've found it. He would have loved to hunt quail in Mexico and perdiz on the plains of Argentina. I don't believe he ever shot one in his life, but hunting ruffed grouse would appeal to him, whether in Minnesota or Nova Scotia, Wisconsin or Ontario. He'd even like driven pheasant in Europe, I suspect, though he would not soon cotton to wearing breeks and a necktie as shooting clothes, and he'd take a while to warm up to the notion of someone loading his gun for him.

Despite such alien customs, he'd recognize the center of the experience instantly, because it's all woven from the same threads. The exquisite beauty of game birds and pointing dogs has little to do with what species they are. You can find the same serenity and sense of place in any hunting fields, whether on the Tisza Plain of Hungary or a cornfield in Iowa. A good gun is a good gun—his Remington 31 pump, my London sidelock, someone else's something else; the man who owns it will love it just as well, no apologies called for, none given.

In my father's world, as in mine, a good shot is a good shot, no matter if he's wearing tweeds or overalls. A sportsman is a gentleman—and if you shot with my father you had damn well better be both.

But this is neither hunting book nor memoir, although as I said, it begins and ends with circumstances that have shaped not only a career but a life as well. Call this instead a celebration of the gun, both as the key element in a lovely sport and for its own sake.

It is by no means the last word on the matter in either case. Dad once told me that no matter what your keenest interest is and no matter how long or how diligently you study, you'll never learn all there is to know about it. He wasn't talking about anything in particular, but the gun is as good an example as any to prove him right. I've been at it for almost thirty years now and sometimes feel as if I've only scratched the surface. That's the fun of it, actually—knowing that if I keep my wits about me and listen well, I'm sure to learn something I don't yet know or see some connection of history or mechanics I haven't recognized before.

Which is not to say I haven't formed certain opinions, or that I haven't changed my mind about some things. Both those phenomena seem to me inevitable results of continued study and learning and thought. You'll find any number of opinions woven into the fabric of these chapters. You may agree with some, disagree with others, and that's fine; this would be a damnably dull world if everyone liked the same things or thought the same way.

I have a notion there's one opinion we all share—that there are few, if any, things in this world more captivating, more compelling, or more thoroughly fascinating than shotguns. Starting with that as our common ground, it seems likely to me that wherever we end up, it won't be far apart.

Michael McIntosh
Copper Creek Farm
Camdenton, Missouri

Acknowledgments

Every chapter in this book first saw the light of day in a magazine. And every issue of every magazine sees the light of day because somewhere behind the scenes there's an editor doing his job. It's a job that earns little glory and less money, but it gets done: magazines get published, and magazine writers thereby earn their daily crust.

I can say without any reservation that shotguns have, in one way or another, introduced me to the best people I know: shooters, readers, colleagues, and friends. My editors—the people who bring my typescripts to print in what to my mind are the finest sporting magazines ever—belong there as well.

As these pieces were first published over quite a span of time, a fair number of people have had a hand in them. Regardless of tenure, they've all believed in my work, and for that I owe an enormous debt of thanks:

To Chuck Wechsler of *Sporting Classics;*

To Steve Smith, Dave Wonderlich, Bill Buckley, and Ralph Stuart, past and present editors of *Shooting Sportsman;*

To Bob Wilbanks of *Gun Dog;*

To Daniel Cote of *The Double Gun Journal.*

There are others, past and present, but these good old sweats are the ones responsible for the stories you'll find here.

That they're here in book form at all is thanks to Jim Rutherford, Charles Fry, Doug Truax, and Art DeLaurier Jr. of

Countrysport Press. Together, they've given me as comfortable a publishing home as any writer ever had.

I owe at least as many thanks, possibly more, to all the people who've taught me something about guns and shooting. But I'm afraid the list of names would be longer than the book, and even then incomplete. So I'll only say: Thanks, lads. You helped me more than most of you ever knew.

Part I

SHOTGUNS

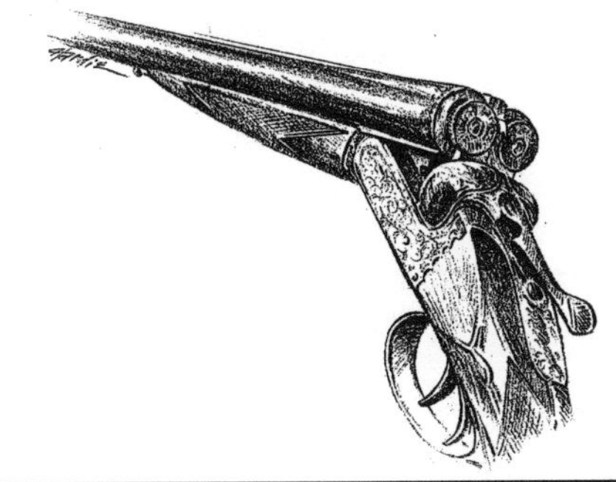

LOVE, LORE, AND LEGEND

LOVE

1

True Confessions

I've often wondered how many people have felt the first sparks of a lifelong passion from an item of household decor. I wonder this because it's happened to me.

It goes way back, this thing with double guns. It started simply as a thing for guns, but whether it originated in nature or nurture, I cannot decide.

On the nurture side, my father was a hunter—of squirrels with a .22 rifle, of quail and pheasant with the dog and gun. He appreciated guns but mainly, I believe, as a means of access to nature. Shooting always was a secondary pleasure, not nearly as important to him as simply being there. A fishing rod served his purpose just as well. Dad told me that he had done some trapshooting in younger days, but I never saw him fire a shot at a clay target.

I inherited Dad's profound love of nature and, indeed, now spend more time afield armed with a walking stick than with a gun.

So I am not the all-around sportsman on whom the typical outdoor magazine predicates editorial policy. Nor do I fit even the readership profile of most gun magazines, no longer eager to plow through articles on anything that shoots.

Which isn't to say I didn't start that way. Wherever the fascination came from, it was there early on.

One of the earliest things I remember is being downtown with my father, looking at some studio photographer's window display. I don't know how old I was, but I was young enough still for Dad to scoop me up in one arm so we could talk face to face, so it must have been the late 1940s. At any rate, that studio window was grandly appealing, a cowboy tableau of sorts—a couple of straw bales, a saddle, lariat, maybe a pair of boots, and, to my eye the centerpiece of it all, a lever-action rifle.

I asked Dad what kind of gun that was, and I can still hear his voice saying, "That's a Marlin."

Well, when you're four or five years old, you don't know Marlin from diddly. Or at least I didn't. I was asking a generic question, but neither of us realized that, so for some time thereafter I thought of any lever-action as a "Marlin."

And I thought about it a lot, not just Marlins but bolt-actions and pump guns and pistols and anything else that stood likely to go bang. I went nowhere, I'm told, without my trusty cap pistols slung low on my hips in the image of Roy and Gene and Hoppy and Johnny Mack Brown. I even wore them to the doctor's office the day my tonsils and I parted company, but that's another story.

At some point, Dad taught me to shoot his .22 and gave me a BB gun. About a year later, presumably convinced I had my head sufficiently wired to handle the thing safely, he gave some BBs to go with it.

I was a great reader by then, but gun magazines weren't in the repertoire. There weren't more than one or two in existence at the time, and in any case I don't believe Dad ever read one until I started writing for them. No, such gun lore as I got in those years came down as tribal knowledge, passed along in the oral tradition from the elders of the clan. Not that guns, or even hunting, were prime topics of conversation at family gatherings or among my father and his friends, but the subject came up often enough, and I homed in with ears sensitive as sonar.

Thirty-ought-six was the first phrase that ever struck my ear as poetry. I don't remember the context, since there weren't many riflemen in southeastern Iowa at the time and probably still aren't, but I loved the crisp, lyric sound of it. Still do.

My grandfather, who even then hadn't hunted for thirty years or more, liked to tell the story of Charley Burton and the Old Belgian Gun, liked to tell it almost as well as I liked to hear it. The gun was Granddad's, on loan to the hired man for a rabbit hunt, and the gist of the tale was that the Old Belgian Gun kicked so hard that one of the hammer spurs gouged a furrow in said Mr. Burton's cheek. End of story.

It was enough. I spent much time wishing the Old Belgian Gun were still around. I was sure I could handle it better than Charley Burton had.

Or maybe not. I wasn't doing all that well with Granddad's little single-shot .410. By the time I was about eleven I had a grand total of one quail to my credit, although the sight of that single bird, one moment streaking down the railroad tracks that bisected the farm and crumpling over the skinny gunbarrel the next, is as clear now as it was then. Rabbits and squirrels were dead meat, by and large, but getting that triple-damned half-ounce of No. 6 shot to intersect the flight line of anything dressed in feathers was beyond me.

There's no telling how many boys have given up shooting forever because of the .410-bore. I find it a frustrating little bitch of a thing, even now, and cringe whenever some well-meaning but ill-guided father drags his kid to the gun club and hands him a .410. It's bad news for beginners.

My own resolve apparently was made of sterner stuff,

stern enough, at least, that I held on until biology came to the rescue and gave me enough growth to convince Dad that I was big enough to handle a real gun.

First it was his Remington pump, a Model 31, one of the silkiest repeating actions ever built. He could shuck three rounds through it so smoothly that the first bird scarcely hit the ground before the third one died. I loved it, mainly because I could actually hit something with it, and I love it still, mainly because it was Dad's gun.

Then he came up with a 16-gauge autoloader, another Remington, a Model 11-48. It was supposed to be mine, I think, but Dad took a shine to it and for a few seasons we sort of swapped it back and forth. That was okay with me. I shot the 12-bore pump better anyway; I never got used to all that machinery rattling around inside the gun every time I pulled the trigger; and somebody had installed a Poly-Choke the size of a goiter out on the business end. By then I'd figured out the advantage of watching the bird instead of the gunbarrel, but I'd usually end up looking at the damn steam-whistle instead.

Good enough pieces, both of them, but neither was the gun I wanted. I wanted a double. And that story starts with a table lamp.

The summer before I was born, Dad won his flight in a local golf tournament and brought home a table lamp as the prize. I don't know how it went over with my mother, but Dad thought it was great, and so, some years later, did I. The lamp was a two-foot shotgun replica, cast of pot-metal and bronzed, its butt resting on a round mahogany base, a fitting for bulbs and a shade attached to the barrels. I thought it was the niftiest thing I'd ever seen. I have it now, and it still gives me a warm feeling when I look at it.

This was no mechanical wonder. This was a gun, a little Parkerlike in some ways but basically a generic sort of double. Now that I have some perspective, it's clear that whoever made the mold it was cast in knew something about double guns, because the shape and the proportions are exactly right. Considering that I was half mad about guns to begin with, it's no wonder I was fascinated by it, but this thing had a quality that affected me as no others did.

It was beautiful.

It had symmetry and grace and a slender elegance like nothing I had ever seen before. Other guns captured my attention because they made me think of cowboys or pheasants or my father; this one was beautiful in its own right, attractive for its own sake, profound in the organic harmony of its curves and planes. I knew of nothing more lovely.

Had Judgment Day come around any time between about 1949 and 1967, I would have gone down instantly on a Covetousness rap. Covetousness in the first degree, with premeditation and avarice aforethought. I've never been so guilty of anything nor embraced a failing with wilder abandon. I wanted a double gun, and the more I learned, the more I wanted one.

By high school, I was pretty well over my hankering for cowboy gear (helped along by actually getting to shoot a .30-30 Winchester). I'd discovered the various gun magazines and read each issue with such absorption that I can still quote some lines and phrases from them after more than twenty-five years. There was a period still ahead when I would be infatuated with rifles and handguns, but the double gun remained the single constant thread. No particular gun, just the idea of the double, the concept of something built to perform one simple function at optimal perfection, something intended, moreover, to combine beauty and efficiency, function and form at levels scarcely paralleled in human experience.

I didn't think of it in those terms then, of course. I had no perspective, no experience from which to discriminate. There were, to my mind, no such things as good doubles and bad ones; if it had two barrels, it was great, so far as I was concerned.

Something else I didn't have in those days was money, nor had I yet discovered the trading game—which was just as well, because my father would have given birth to a brick if I'd swapped off any of the family guns. (He thought I was out of my mind even years later, when I traded the old Remington autoloading 16—possession of which was by then solely mine—for an L.C. Smith 20. Dad, I'm afraid, never could quite understand why anyone would want something as old-fashioned as a gun with two barrels and two triggers when he could have a repeater.)

Anyway, like most adolescent males, my life was a constant round of scheming for ways to obtain the two things I wanted most in the world, one of which was a double gun. I never passed up an opportunity to fondle, covet, drool over, or shoot any double I saw. I can't, even now, very accurately describe the feeling I got from having one in my hands, but I imagine you know what I'm talking about. One of Dad's hunting partners owned a 20-gauge Browning Superposed, and he was kind enough to let me carry it for a while every time we hunted together. Over-unders never have moved me in quite the same aesthetic ways that side-by-sides do, but I looked upon that little Browning much the way I regarded the centerfolds in Playboy; whatever the difference, it was merely a matter of kind, not degree.

Superposed Brownings and Playmates of the Month struck me as being about equally attainable, too. Brownings, after all, cost nearly $400 in those days.

As it will do, college distracted me enough that my double-gun passion dropped from a rolling boil to a simmer, while I concentrated on laying the foundation of what would be my career for quite a few years after. September 1967 was the turning point. I was a senior, living off-campus for the first time and therefore able to take my gun to school without the inconvenience of storing it elsewhere. Sometime during the first week of classes, I dropped by the local gunshop, intending nothing more than an hour of browsing, and left as the owner of a double gun.

Co-owner, actually. I never knew whether Maurice LeMaster took pity on me or just got tired of handing over the same three or four guns for my weekly fondling-and-drooling fix, but either way, he was a nice man. The upshot was that he got claim to every spare penny I could scrape together over the next six months, and I got a 20-gauge double.

It was a Stevens Model 311, one of the older ones that showed at least a hint of old-fashioned workmanship. It wasn't much, but it was mine, and that was plenty. I doubt I've ever lavished as much pure love on any gun. If I picked it up now, it'd feel like a fencepost; then, it felt like a dream.

I had some instinct for shooting, but instinct was about all. I thought you were supposed to hold a splinter fore-end by the wood, for God's sake. Nevertheless, I took my new old Stevens out the next afternoon, killed a barnyard pigeon with the first shot, and though I didn't know it at the time, changed my life forever.

I haven't been without at least one double gun since. In the following autumn, taking a year off to put together some money for graduate school and a bit extra for fooling with guns, I discovered the trading game and went, to put it mildly, out of my mind, a condition that lasted the better part of ten years. I traded for anything and everything, with anybody who'd hold still for a little dickering and with quite a few who wouldn't.

Like a monk suddenly released from his vows, I determined to make up for lost time and own, however briefly, every double gun I could get my hands on. I still couldn't afford much, but looking back, I think I did okay for a kid without many loose dollars. Really fine foreign guns and high-grade American doubles were out of the question, of course, but somehow I managed to own at least one specimen of nearly all the good ones and quite a few that weren't so good. I seldom could afford to have more than two or three at the same time, but that didn't matter; almost every one of them was exactly what I wanted until the next one came along.

My first really good double was an L.C. Smith, a late-production Field Grade 20 built on the Featherweight frame. For it, I traded a nearly new Savage Fox Model B 20-bore, the old Remington 16-gauge, and ten bucks "boot." Somebody had refinished the stock by painting it with thick, black varnish, and when I stripped that away, I found a gorgeous piece of fiddleback walnut. It was unquestionably factory wood, but I've never believed it was wood meant for a Field Grade. Some factory stocker apparently screwed up, and I got a lucky break.

The more guns I handled, the clearer my concept of quality became. At first virtually any gun would do, so long as it had two barrels. Then for a while I was fascinated by fancy engraving (not good, just fancy) and by such features as beavertail fore-ends, single triggers, vent ribs, and ejectors. I hung onto the little Smith 20 for several years and from it began to develop a notion of quality that had little to do with ornamentation and nothing at all to do with the add-on extras. I began, in short, to understand something of design and craftsmanship and performance. From that point, with only occasional backsliding, I began to want guns that were better than I was, a step beyond whatever my concept of high quality was at the time. I wanted each one to be more beautiful than the last, either in sheer design, in execution, or handling. I wanted guns that challenged my ability to appreciate them.

I also wanted to learn everything I could about double guns, how they're conceived, how they're built, how they work, who made them and why. By then, the early 1970s, I was teaching literature at a small state college in Missouri, developing a career from the serious study of the greatest products of the human spirit, and I began, slowly at first, to see that in some serious and important ways, truly fine guns are as much works of art as poems, novels, paintings, symphonies, or plays. This is not generally the cultural view of guns, but social approbation never has been the measure of true quality in most things.

One important lesson remained. About 1971, I saved up as much cash as I could possibly justify spending on a gun ($400) and bought a VH Grade Parker 16, mostly because I was hopelessly enthralled by the Parker mystique. It was a nice little gun, well-worn but not abused, fitted with 26-inch tubes and a factory single trigger. I figured I had arrived.

True enough. I had arrived at the threshold of one of

the worst experiences I ever had with a gun. The stock was too short and too low in the comb; the chokes were so bloody tight that it shot like a rifle. The gun, in short, fit neither me nor the kind of shooting I wanted to do with it. Those gun-of-the-month trading years were the absolute nadir of my shooting ability, probably worse than the time I served behind Granddad's .410. Why is no great mystery, since I was using a different gun just about every time I went out, but none of it came even close to the misery I went through with that Parker.

I kept it three years, unable to admit that a specimen of the lordly and legendary Parker was anything but the perfect gun. The fact is, there was nothing wrong with the gun, only with me. I didn't understand until much later, long after I finally sold the damn thing, that I expected things of the gun that should have come from myself, and vice versa. I had clung to it for the wrong reasons, more in love with the idea of owning a Parker than clear-headed enough to see that it wasn't the Parker for me.

Collectors and shooters see guns from different angles. To the one, fit and function are hardly important; to the other, they are vital. But to both, to all of us, the gun is greater than the sum of its parts. It is a thing of resounding implications, a connection among spirits of those who've gone before and those who will come after. I've found something to like about nearly every gun I ever owned, but I learned the hard way to be choosy about the ones I allow to steal my heart.

With that, the frenetic round of swap and acquisition began to fade. Owning and studying a few hundred guns over a period of years is a good way to develop some technical savvy and personal tastes. I'm still interested, academically at least, in virtually anything with two barrels, but those I actually own and shoot are few. By far the majority of my early work was with American guns, and I've come to recognize some favorites. I find Lefevers, both versions, highly appealing mechanically, and Parkers charm my aesthetic sense. Foxes satisfy my tastes for both mechanics and art better than any.

But it's a big world, that of the double, and in recent

years I've begun to study the history and products of the European trade. At the moment, I'm most interested in guns from the golden age of the English trade, from about 1875 to World War II, and in the current Italian makers, particularly Piotti, Fabbri, Bertuzzi, Marocchi, Rizzini, and Zanotti. My personal battery is minuscule compared with what it used to be. I shoot targets with a Marocchi Contrast, game with an old B Grade Fox and a London sidelock built in the 1930s by John Wilkes. There are a couple of others, pieces that appeal to me for one reason or another and serve some specific purposes, but those three are the heart of my gunning these days.

Which isn't to say that the Acquisitive Kid is dead and gone. I can think of about two dozen makers worldwide whose guns I'd love to own. The stakes are considerably higher now, and if the Kid ever again got the upper hand, I'd soon be threadbare and living on roadkill and dog food in the back of my Blazer.

But I'd have a hell of a collection of double guns to watch by the light of a funny old lamp.

2

Honey and Smoke

With the possible exceptions of cotton and concrete, there is scarcely a substance on earth that hasn't at least been tried as material for gunstocks. Stocks have been carved from ivory, cast of metals base and precious, molded from polymers, cobbled up from Lord knows what—even laminated from buffalo horn.

Wood, of course, is the most successful substance, but even then, the list of what's been tried isn't much shorter than a list of what's available—everything from oak to pine, birch to beech, mesquite to maple to myrtle to madrone, persimmon, pecan, holly, teak, mahogany, and such exotic African species as kokrodua, ekki, ebony, benge, bubinga, sifou, sapele, and some others with equally weird names. Most of these woods are perfectly serviceable for stocks, but ultimately, none can hold a candle to walnut. For gunstock wood, walnut is the king, the classic, the daisy, the pearl, the star.

Walnut is hard and strong, stable, lightweight, shock-resistant, flexible—probably courteous and reverent besides. It shrinks and swells less than almost any other wood. It's sweet to work, lovely to smell, delightful to handle, and takes a splendid finish. And walnut is without question the most extraordinarily beautiful wood on earth, ranging from the color of honey to the rich depth of chocolate-brown, often marked with smoky swirls and streaks of pigment from dark brown to black. The grain can be perfectly straight, elegantly swept, or a festival of waves, curls, mottles and motes, sunburst and fiddleback, as intricate as an opium dream. You can get lost in the texture of walnut.

Which is not to say that all walnut is created equal. Color and figure varies from species to species, tree to tree, even among parts of the same tree. Density, hardness, and working characteristics also vary, particularly from one species to another.

Walnuts belong to the genus *Juglans*, which comprises forty-odd species worldwide. Most are about equally desirable for cabinets, furniture, and veneer, but for gunstock wood, some are decidedly more desirable than others. *Juglans regia*, as its name suggests, is the aristocrat of them all. This is Old World or European walnut, variously called English, French, Spanish, Circassian, Turkish, Persian, Himalayan, or by some other name, according to where it grows. American black walnut, *J. nigra*, is endemic to eastern North America and was taken west by the pioneers.

California and Hinds walnuts—technically *J. californica* and *J. hindsii* but commonly called Claro—are native to the West. European walnut grows there, too, transplanted about a hundred years ago following failed attempts to raise it commercially in the East and South. This in turn led to a couple of man-made species, at least one of which is used for gunstocks. Bastogne is a hybrid cross between European and Hinds walnuts. Why it's named after a town in southeastern Belgium, I'm not sure, except that the Ardennes Forest region traditionally was a source of fine stock wood. (I doubt it has anything at all to do with the fact that American Brigadier General Anthony McAuliffe, surrounded at Bastogne by the German Army in 1944 and asked to surrender, replied simply, "Nuts!") At any rate, Bastogne walnut combines the characteristics of its parent stock—the intricate, predominantly fiddleback figure of Claro and the warm color of European.

Each species has its own peculiar physical identity. American walnut is densest and hardest of all. A one-foot cube of it, with moisture content at 12 percent, weighs 38 pounds, 5 pounds heavier than a similar cube of *J. regia.* In the standard hardness test, 1,010 pounds of pressure is required to embed a .444-inch steel ball to half its diameter in a slab of black walnut; 860 pounds will do the same to a piece of Old World wood.

Stocks made of black walnut are sturdy, durable, and range from plain to nicely figured. The American arms industry turns them out by the zillion every year. Stockmakers, however, don't like black walnut as well as *J. regia.* Jack Rowe, an English stocker who now lives in Oklahoma, puts it this way: "It doesn't work so nicely as the French wood, and it doesn't smell as good either."

Black walnut has at least one practical disadvantage besides. It's stiffer and therefore doesn't flex under recoil the way European walnut does. This isn't a problem with rifles, so long as the actions are solidly bedded and perhaps even fitted with recoil lugs, because rifle stocks usually are fairly chunky in the wrist. Nor is it much of a problem for a shotgun stock attached by a drawbolt. But black walnut worked to the slender proportions of a fine game gun and attached via the traditional tang screws is almost certain to develop a cracked wrist sooner or later—or a cracked head, à la L.C. Smith, because the wrist is unable to dampen the shock.

Claro often shows lovely color and striking figure, but it's the softest of all the gunstock walnuts. The open grain and comparatively pulpy texture make it the least suitable stock wood from a functional standpoint. Recoil stress can compress it over time and thereby loosen the fit between wood and metal.

Sharply pointed, fine-line hand checkering is extremely hard to accomplish with Claro; about all you get is a crosshatch of fuzzy gouges.

Fiddleback figure, characteristic of both Claro and Bastogne, is certainly handsome to the eye, but it can be frustrating for a stockmaker. Since fiddleback runs across the basic grain of the wood, it often wants to chip rather than take a clean cut from an inletting chisel. Jack Rowe voices what seems to be a majority opinion when he talks about the working character of Claro and Bastogne: "You get bits and corners flying out when you're inletting; it's awful stuff. Awful stuff." The climate where it grows affects walnut profoundly. In cool climates, where the annual growing season is short, trees produce harder, denser wood, with growth rings more closely spaced. Consequently, the most desirable black walnut comes from the northern states—Minnesota, Iowa, New York, Pennsylvania. Climate is a function of altitude as well as latitude, and the finest of all gunstock wood traditionally has come from the Central Massif of France; from the Ardennes; from the Circassian region of the northwestern Caucasus along the Black Sea; and from the highlands of Turkey and Iran. Ironically, the one place that never has produced particularly good Old World walnut is England, though we persist in thinking of European walnut generically as "English." Although they're the same botanically, Old World trees show certain regional characteristics, or so W. W. Greener insists. French wood, he tells us, is lighter-weight, more open-grained and more richly colored than English wood. German and Swiss walnut is pulpy, soft and gray; Italian wood heavy and bland in background color. Some stockmakers consider Old World walnut grown in California to be harder and more brittle than the same species grown elsewhere.

You can make a gunstock from any part of a walnut tree that can yield a proper-sized chunk—even a limb, although limb wood tends to be less stable (that is, more likely to warp) than wood from thicker parts. Stock blanks cut from sections where the trunk forks or where main branches meet the trunk often show an elaborate sunburst figure generally called "feathered crotch." The best wood, however, comes from the base, from the root section up to about six feet above ground-level. There, especially where the roots join the trunk, the wood is densest and most beautifully figured. To describe a particularly handsome stock as "a fine hunk of stump" isn't entirely an exercise in folksy slang.

In order to obtain the root section, the business of harvesting a walnut tree is a matter of grubbing up rather than cutting down. In this country nowadays it's done by machine, especially on large-scale commercial plantations. In the old days, it was everywhere done by hand, and in many parts of the world, it still is. In regions where naturally grown walnut has been harvested for generations, suitable trees inevitably have become scarcer and their locations more remote, so that even now in the Near and Middle East, as elsewhere, machinery often is little more than a supplement to muscle and sweat.

We think of the stockmaker as the key figure in producing a fine gunstock. Actually he is but one in a series of master craftsmen who contribute to the process and whose work must complement one another's if the results are to be fully successful.

The sawyer is the first of them. Once out of the ground and trimmed, the trees are taken to local sawmills where the bark is removed and the logs sawn into slabs about three inches thick. The sawyer's work is critical, because the angle at which wood is cut relative to the annular or growth rings of the log determines much of its ultimate appearance. Slab-sawing, in which the sawblade is basically parallel to the grain, reveals one sort of figure; quarter-sawing, in which the blade is angled across the growth rings, reveals another.

Both methods can produce lovely results, but by the same token, either method can turn a potentially gorgeous piece of wood into something as dull as cardboard. It all depends upon the tree and upon how skillfully the sawyer can read the grain before he cuts.

The marker, too, is a master of his craft. His job is to examine the rough-sawn planks and determine exactly how each one will be further cut into stock blanks. One of the marker's objectives is to get the maximum number of stocks out of each plank, but he must be concerned with quality and usefulness as well. Highly figured wood is attractive, but in practical terms, location of the figure is more important than looks.

A gunstock has to absorb a considerable amount of stress and strain, especially in the head, where it meets the metal, and in the wrist or hand, where a stock is thinnest. Since wood cracks along its grain, it's extremely important that the grain structure in the head and hand be able to provide maximum strength and flexibility—and elaborate, curly grain does not meet that prescription. Ideally, the grain should run straight and parallel through the hand and head, especially in a stock attached by tang screws; the figure, all or most, should be farther back where it's displayed to best advantage and at the same time doesn't interfere with functional quality.

The marker knows all this, and he patterns out each plank into blanks that show the best possible combination of beauty and strength. He may have to sacrifice a stock or two to achieve optimum quality, but the ones he does get will fetch a higher price in the end.

The marker also patterns his planks to avoid defects that sawing has revealed—cracks, wind-shakes, knots, and the like. He tries to avoid sapwood, which is the softer, lighter-colored portion of the log nearest the surface. Sapwood is not necessarily inferior, and it can be stained to match the rest, but true best-quality stocks come entirely from heartwood, nearest the core of the log.

After the marker has done his work, the wood must be dried—either as planks or, more typically, as blanks. Freshly cut wood is full of moisture, both sap and water. Moisture content may be as high as 90 percent, present both as free water and bound water. Free water is in the veins, pores, capillaries, and cell cavities, and it leaves quickly. Bound water is trapped in the interior structure of the wood itself and takes considerably longer to evaporate.

Walnut cannot be properly worked until the moisture content is down to about 12 percent. Otherwise, it will shrink and warp as it dries. Stock wood traditionally is air-dried, stored away in some protected place and allowed to season for about six years before it's sold to gunmakers. Some gunmakers, in turn, dry it even longer.

In this century, some wood merchants in France and Turkey have found a way of accelerating the drying process. Once the planks are patterned and cut, they seal the ends of the blanks, place them in a pit and steam them to drive out the sap. The remaining moisture apparently can be sufficiently evaporated in about a year.

American wood dealers generally prefer kiln-drying, arguing that it's the only way to achieve consistent, predictable results, and that it does so in minimum time besides. There are kilns and kilns, of course, and a wood-drying kiln is neither blast furnace nor bake-oven; rather, it's an enclosed chamber in which temperature, humidity, and airflow can be precisely controlled and where dehumidification generally takes place at less than a hundred degrees Fahrenheit.

In either method, the objective is not only to reduce moisture content but to do so from the inside out and to make it consistent throughout the blank. If free water is allowed to leave too quickly, the wood surface literally case-hardens, forming a hard, shriveled, cracked skin that effectively prevents internal moisture from ever getting out—or at least keeps it inside until a stockmaker removes the outer skin, at which point he's dealing with wet wood that will either warp or rust the metal parts attached to it, or both. Discovering fine lockwork pitted with rust from wood that was too moist does not make happy gun owners.

Because stockmaking, like every other fine craft, has a highly subjective side, stockers disagree over the relative merits of kiln- and air-drying. American craftsmen seem about equally divided on the matter, but to a man, all of the Old World-trained stockmakers I know prefer their wood air-dried. They all say kiln-dried wood seems more brittle.

Trained at Purdey's, David Trevallion has for nearly thirty years plied his craft in America. Specializing in best-quality English and European guns, he has worked with some of the finest walnut put on guns in the latter twentieth century. He speculates that kiln-drying may remove more natural oil than air-drying does. "I notice it most in checkering," he says, "especially at twenty-six or twenty-eight lines per inch or finer. Kiln-dried wood seems to chip more, while a properly air-dried piece will take thirty or thirty-two lines quite well."

One thing everyone agrees upon is that best-quality walnut is hard to come by. Apparently it always has been, since Greener, writing in 1910, remarks that "the amount of really fine wood available is limited."

It is sometimes a wonder that really fine wood is available at all, considering how much is lost to a whole range of ills, from disease and damage in harvest and hauling, to faulty sawing and improper drying. And then there's the matter of supply.

In climates that produce the best wood, walnut trees take seventy-five years or more to reach a size worth harvesting. And they've been cut for fenceposts and building lumber, burned as firewood, turned into military rifle stocks, and, especially in Europe, blown to splinters in two enormously destructive wars during this century alone. Gunmakers are only now beginning to feel the pinch from trees devastated during the 1914–1918 war; effects of the even greater carnage wreaked on European forests from 1939 to 1945 are still twenty years in the future.

Turkey and Iran continue to supply a fair amount of walnut, but for the most part, fine walnut stock blanks from the traditional sources are dwindling. Teyssier, the French company in Brive la Gaillarde that once supplied the London gun trade with wood that everyone calls the best of the best, has, I believe, recently closed down. Those who have the goods are selling ever more dearly—upwards of $700 per blank in this country (often considerably upwards) and £1,000 or more in London, for top-quality stuff. A perfectly matched set of blanks for a matched pair of guns commands a premium price, $4,000 or more.

This is not to say that all the world's resources of walnut have been tapped. Such relatively untapped sources as Pakistan and South America and China, which probably has walnut trees by the million, are either unreliable or unavailable. Wood from yet other places—Australia and New Zealand, for instance—is for one reason or another less desirable. Australian walnut tends to be extremely heavy; New Zealand wood suffers an unusually high number of wind-shakes—cracks inflicted when the tree was young enough to be flexed and twisted by high winds.

There isn't much use wailing over spilt milk or wasted walnut, but it seems a shame nonetheless that we don't truly appreciate something until it's hard to find. I don't bear furniture people any ill-will, but I do tend to see lost gunstocks in every fine walnut desk or table or cabinet. Worse yet, I've seen some rusty, beat-up old military rifles stocked with pieces of European walnut that could bring tears to the eyes of a dead snake.

On the other hand, a graceful game gun stocked with elegantly figured wood the color of honey and smoke is an almost tearful thing as well, but the feeling is different. It's a reminder that man and nature aren't always at odds, that sometimes, when human craft and the artistry of nature coincide, the result can take hold of your heart.

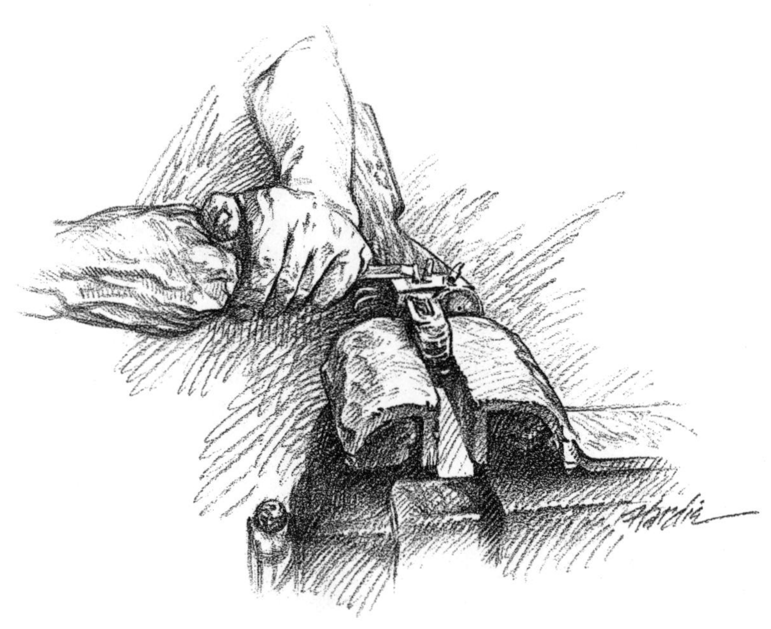

3

Wizardry in Walnut

David Trevallion's workbenches are a sort of working monument to tradition. At first glance, they're just files and chisels, ranked and racked amid an orderly clutter of mallets and turnscrews, drawknives and spokeshaves, kerosene wicks, saws and pliers and scribers and gauges and gizmos—tools of the stockmaker's trade. Take a closer look, and history begins to show, as on the checkered walnut breastpiece of a gunmaker's brace with "David Trevallion, July '59" inlaid in silver wire.

"That's the date I finished my apprenticeship at Purdey's," David says. "Ken Hunt, who'd just recently finished his engraving apprenticeship with Harry Kell, helped me with the inlay."

Other tools go much farther back. David's bend-jig, used to measure the drop dimensions of a gunstock, belonged to Purdey stockmaker Cornelius Deane in the latter part of the nineteenth century, and then to his son Philip, who started working at Purdey's in 1909. "When Phil died, Harry Lawrence divided up some of his tools between me and another apprentice. The old thing's measured a lot of stocks, that's for sure."

Some of the chisels and gouges on David's bench have seen a lot of stocks, too; they've been in use for a hundred years or more, passed down among generations of Purdey craftsmen. And they're still in use, day by day, still working fine walnut into gunstocks.

For so old a tradition, the actual process has been given surprisingly little treatment in print—even from the old-timers who went on at great length to describe everything else about gunmaking. Of 780-odd pages in the final edition of *The Gun*, W.W. Greener devotes fewer than a dozen to stockmaking, and most of those are taken up with discussions of how to measure length and cast. John Henry Walsh gives stockmaking equally short shrift in *The Modern Sportsman's Gun and Rifle*—exactly five pages out of nearly five hundred—and summarizes the whole process by saying that the stockmaker's task is "to insert the action in a piece of walnut wood properly seasoned."

Well, if that's all there is to it, no wonder stockmaking seems the most accessible of all the various wizardries involved in creating a fine gun. Think about it: How many home-workshop tinkerers do you know who've tried building a set of barrels or filing up a pair of locks? But doesn't it seem, on the other hand, that just about everybody who ever successfully knocked together a birdhouse has had a go at making a gunstock? I have, and I'll bet you have, too. I imagine we know about fifty guys who've done the same.

Shaped and pre-inletted wood from Fajen and Bishop confers a fair chance of success to all but the most ham-handed of amateurs. But this is not stockmaking, any more than a paint-by-number canvas is a piece of art. Real stockmaking begins with a walnut blank and ends with an elegant sculpture that looks as if it grew from the steel. What happens betweentimes requires craftsmanship of the highest order, and the result is art of a rarefied form.

Which is not to minimize anyone's contribution, because without first-class work all the way from barrelmaker to finisher, you can't have a best-quality gun. Nonetheless, the stockmaker is responsible for at least half the beauty and something more than half the practical function. Metal men, as the old adage goes, make a gun fire, but the stocker makes it shoot.

Exactly how he does so depends to some extent upon where he learned the craft, for different gunmakers approach stockmaking in slightly different ways, each according to his own sense of procedure, style, and proportion. It's a process guided by tradition and, at its best, governed by standards in which only the highest-quality work is acceptable.

Because it's a story worth the telling, midsummer took me to the coast of Maine to watch and photograph the business of stockmaking by a master craftsman, performed according to the traditional precepts of the trade.

David Trevallion, Freeman of the Society of Gunmakers of the City of London and formerly of James Purdey & Sons, was fifteen years old when he began his apprenticeship at Purdey's, under the tutelage of master stockmaker William O'Brien. "David got up to just as much mischief as any apprentice," Bill, who is now retired, told me over lunch in London last spring, "but I could see early on that he had a special talent for the work which a lot of apprentices, even many who go on to become quite successful, don't have."

You can see as much in any Trevallion stock, if you know what to look for, and there are plenty of them to see, because he's been at it in this country since he arrived here in April 1964. In the years we've been friends, I've watched him do any number of little jobs and briefly watched gunstocks progress through this stage or that. But this would be the first time I'd see the work from beginning to end—and for the first time, the gun in question was mine.

David thinks I should own a Purdey (he thinks everyone should own a Purdey), and I certainly would if I could afford one. As it is, I'm happy with my 1930s-vintage best-quality John Wilkes. Even though the original stock had been lengthened and bent to a reasonably good fit, an old repair behind the right-hand lockplate was starting to give out, making clear that a choice was in the offing—either go for another repair or have a new stock made. Given the prospect of dressing a gun I dearly love with a stock tailor-made by a craftsman whose work I so admire—it wasn't a difficult choice at all.

We spent the first evening deciding on the wood and the dimensions. David's inventory of blanks turned up a piece of walnut with just the sort of smoky, streaky figure I find most appealing, a blank bearing the stamp of Teyssier, the old French wood merchant whose wares the London trade once called "the best of the best." A grease-penciled legend on the end showed that David bought it in 1983.

Using a transparent template in the shape of a gunstock, David marked the blank to establish optimum grain-pattern in the hand and head, weighed it (four pounds, three ounces), and set it aside.

For the next hour, we worked on the fit, taking measurements from the old stock and revising them step by step. Again and again, he put me through the drill: mount and point—at his eye, over his shoulder, at a spot on the wall, here and there. We finished up using a Spot Shot, a nifty little flashlight that fits into a gunbarrel; when you pull the trigger, a teacup-sized patch of light shows exactly where the barrel's pointing.

I hadn't been measured for a stock in quite a few years, and our bodies do change over time. Jack Mitchell, who's done more for my shooting than all the instructors I ever met put together, told me a good while back that I was due for something longer than the 14⅝-inch stocks I've been using since I was about thirty, and now David gradually built up the length with a slip-on boot and spacers until it felt just right—at a surprising 15¼ inches from the front trigger to the center of the butt. David suggested reducing the pitch for more uniform contact between the butt and my shoulder, and since a good part of what was pectoral-muscle mass when I was thirty now resides considerably closer to my belt, I had to agree. At least the drops and my old half-inch cast at heel were still good, to which David added an eighth-inch more twist at the toe to fit the slant of my shoulder.

As a final check, he clamped the gun to his setting bench, turned on the heat lamps, and bent the old stock to the new dimensions. "We could set this up on my try-gun," he said, "but it's a different weight and balance, and I prefer to check things out on the gun that's actually getting the new stock. Fewer surprises that way."

Unlike some things in life, it felt just as good next morning as it had the night before, so David began marking up the blank, measuring and scribing centerlines and other marks to guide the initial cuts.

"The trick," he said, "is to let in the top-strap at a proper depth and angle so the bend and cast dimensions will be right when I bring the head up against the frame. I suppose you could fit the frame straight in and try to adjust everything by bending the wood later, but that doesn't always work. I was taught it's best to build the dimensions in right from the start."

The first cut, a freehand pass on the bandsaw along a carefully drawn line, establishes the top contour of the stock, a gentle curve from the head down the top of the wrist, a sharper curve up where the comb rises (called the thumbhole in the English trade), and then straight back to the heel. A second cut, across the front end, sets the angle for the cast. So much for power tools.

"Now," David said, "when I let the top-strap down to the level of the wood, a level I've predetermined with the first cut, both bend and cast should be right on the dot, so the first stage of inletting is also the first stage of shaping—on the top side, from the action face all the way back to the heel. As I gradually let the head up, I'll have to be careful to bring it up perfectly straight and not allow it to twist; if it does, the cast gets all screwed up."

By now, my gun is long since in pieces, locks and trigger plate off, old stock removed, and all parts out of the frame—top lever, spindle, bolt, cocking levers, firing pins, springs, safety, everything. David will reassemble it bit by bit, removing wood to accommodate each piece in turn.

The first order of business is the frame itself, and a good fit here is essential, both to achieve proper dimensions and to keep the gun functioning at its best. Unless the frame is in solid contact with the head of the stock, recoil will soon crack and split the wood, bringing the whole job—and the stockmaker's reputation—to ruin. Sidelock guns of English design have more bearing surface at the head than sidelocks are generally thought to have, but a good stockmaker is nonetheless careful to use every square millimeter of it and to make certain that every point of contact is uniformly snug. Since he's literally working in three dimensions, it's a slow, complex task.

Six hours after David made the first chisel cut to start the top-strap down, the wood was fully mated to the frame—six hours of patient shaving and slicing, of continually reblacking the metal with smoke from a kerosene wick, checking constantly with a steel thumbhole gauge laid across the top of the frame and down over the tang, slowly deepening the tang at the rear to bring up the bend, fitting and cutting bit by tiny bit. At one point, I picked off a shaving he'd just cut from the top-strap channel and out of curiosity measured it with a dial indicator. Three-thousandths of an inch, about the thickness of cheap, lightweight typing paper. I've taken lifelong pleasure in making things myself, especially from wood, so next time David took a break, I tried my hand at getting up a shaving equally thin. Ten-thousandths was the best I could do.

When he's satisfied that everything fits the way it should, he slides the frame onto the wood, raps the breech face lightly with the heel of his hand, and steel and wood come together with an audible click.

"Bill O'Brien used to do this with the jobs we did, snap it together this way, then take it out of the vise and hold it by the action. If the wood fell off on the floor, he'd say, 'Do it again.' And we'd have to start over, with a new piece of wood—

didn't make Purdey's very happy with their apprentices, I can tell you."

So saying, he spun open the vise and lifted my gun by the action bar, the inletting fit alone holding a four-pound blank firmly to the frame. He shook it a couple of times, and it still didn't budge. "This'll do," David said.

He put it back in the vise, belly-up, and started shaving the bottom of the wrist with a drawknife. "The trigger plate goes in next, and then I can drill the hole for the breech pin and fasten everything together."

The trigger plate, too, is a critical step, partly because it plays a key role in holding the frame to the wood. A portion of it, called the trigger box, projects upward at a slight angle and forms a seat for the breech pin, which is the main tang screw located underneath the top lever. When properly fitted, the angled surface of the trigger box bears against the interior of the stock, and as the breech pin is tightened, the sloped surface, along with the front side of the breech pin itself, draws the frame and stock ever more firmly together.

The depth to which the trigger plate is let in is important as well, because this governs how well the triggers and safety work. If the plate is inlet too deeply, the triggers bear against the sears once the locks are installed, and the gun won't cock; it binds the safety besides. If it's not in deeply enough, the triggers can't reach the sears.

A few more hours of patient work with chisel and gouge, and by next day the trigger plate is in to within a sixteenth-inch of its final depth. "I won't let this all the way in," David said, "until I've fitted the breech pin and hand pin [the rear tang screw], inlet the safety bar and thumb-piece and triggers. That way, I'm leaving myself some latitude to adjust the contact between the triggers and the safety bar, and that adjustment establishes the proper relationship between triggers and sears." In gunmakers' parlance, tension on the breech pin is called "draw." Draw is applied with a brace and a screwdriver-blade bit called a chisel, and the amount is considerable, indeed. It is, after all, what holds the gun together.

"We used to drive the finishers at Purdey's crazy," David says. "We'd put the pins up so hard they couldn't get them out, so they'd have to bring the guns over and ask us to do it. They hated that." As he talks, David is tightening my gun's breech pin for the umpteenth time, having shaved out another microscopic layer of wood. "We used to play tricks on each other, too—put a thin strip of pine on the floor, with one end on a block of wood, and then step on it just as the chap's putting the last bit of draw on a pin, make him think for an instant that he broke it."

Just then, from somewhere in the depths of my beloved Wilkes, comes a snappy little ping. David looks at me.

"I didn't step on anything," I said.

"I know," David said. "Your breech pin just broke. Happens a lot with older guns."

"Christ almighty! First you bleed on my stock, then you break my breech pin. You sure this is how it's done at Purdey's?" (That no Trevallion job is complete until it's blooded is long-standing chaff between us. You should see what he's done to some of my books.)

"Sure. I did it on purpose so you could write about how to make a breech pin—put some flesh on the story."

So we made a breech pin, or rather David made one while I watched. Someday I'll have it engraved to match the old one. Or maybe I won't; it doesn't show, and its shiny blue face reminds me of that day every time I look at it.

"Once years ago, I slipped with a really sharp chisel and cut one of the triggers off a Westley Richards," David said. "Triggers are sometimes quite soft."

"Spare me that, if you don't mind. The story's fleshy enough."

By Saturday morning, beginning of day three, the frame and trigger plate were in and securely pinned; the spindle and bolt were back in place, likewise the safety and triggers, and David had the entire profile shaped. He'd brought the bends right up to a gnat's whisker, cut it to length and shaped the butt according to the geometric layout standard at Purdey's:

the stock belly now showed the trim lines typical of a London best. Ready for locks.

The first step is stripping all the lockwork off the plates. Actually, David explained the sequence and made me do the work, with spring cramps and screwdriver. Dismantling these old locks, made by Joseph Brazier of Wolverhampton, was like taking apart a fine old watch, built to such tolerances that a thin coat of oil makes the parts stick together in a sucking fit.

With more smoke and more shaving, David inlets the plates, working front to back, easing them gradually down to surface-level and just below. And then the lockworks, part by part, sear spring first. The main sear, tumbler, and bridle complete the first stage. Interceptor and interceptor spring come next. Last piece in will be the mainspring.

Meticulously, David removes only enough to accommodate the parts, leaving standing wood between. "Anyplace you can leave wood supporting the plates helps strengthen the whole thing," he says. "But some of it, like here in this little comma-shaped hole in the bridle...the hole itself is purely decorative, and I'll leave a little wooden post that fits it, because the tradition says I should, but the best way to describe it is 'gunmaker's gothic.' It's there to show what a stockmaker can do—even though you'd never see it unless you pulled the locks off.

"The other consideration, obviously, is to have no contact at all between the wood and the moving parts, to leave enough space to let the wood swell a bit in damp weather and still not bind the lockwork. Even so, I don't like to take out any more than necessary. Touchy work."

With the locks finally in place, holes drilled for the firing pins, and everything snugged down and trimmed up to David's satisfaction, we fired the first shots at half-past seven that evening, taking turns blasting rights and lefts at the bullet trap in a corner of the shop. A box of cartridges later, David removes the locks and examines all the inletting and heading to be certain that nothing has moved and that the fit remains tight. Nothing has, and it is. A good day's work.

The wood at this point looks basically like a gunstock—in profile, anyway—but it's still at nearly original thickness and is square-edged everywhere except at the butt. Next morning, David began fitting the trigger guard, which refines the stock belly's profile. It's a surprisingly painstaking, time-consuming affair.

"In a subtle way, the shape of the belly affects a stock's whole appearance," David says. "The line from the back of the trigger-guard bow to the toe ought to be perfectly straight, or even slightly concave. But never convex. If it's the least bit convex, the stock has a heavy, fish-bellied look, not graceful at all. Bloody thing'll look like a pregnant carp.

"The first thing is to get the correct distance between the guard bow and the triggers. Guards are left soft, and they're easy to reshape if necessary. Then you let it in until you can seat the first screw. That holds everything properly in place while you let in the tang.

"From there, you keep checking with a straight-edge gauge and keep letting the tang down until it's seated and the line of the stock belly is right. When it is, you have a profile you can work to in rounding it up."

From the tangs to the butt, shaping calls for planes, a drawknife, various wood files, and a well-practiced ability to cut complex curves while keeping the wood surface free of ripples and dips. "If I have to do the job in a hurry, I can enlist the aid of Colonel Sanders over there," he says, nodding toward his belt sander, "but I prefer shaping it up by hand. The trick with the drawknife is to always work with the grain. That means you have to work each side of a quarter-sawn blank, like this one, in a different direction. Try to cut against the grain, and you take a chance on raising a big sliver, because the grain will pull the blade deeper into the wood than you want. At best, the surface will end up rough rather than smooth."

Between the drawknife and the files, David uses a lovely, old-fashioned little cherrywood spokeshave for touching-up. Another Purdey's piece?

"Actually, no. I'm told this came from the stockmaking shop at the old Parker factory. Nice tool to use." I try it. The blade glides through the wood like butter, and fragrant, paper-thin shavings curl up behind, smoothly, almost hypnotically. Left to myself, I might have gone on shaving until the stock was as slim as the barrels.

David finished the shaping with progressively finer-cut rasps, rounded off the butt, and then checked the balance. With the old stock, the balance point was 1⅞ inches forward of the breech face, and I wanted to keep it there. The standard method of balancing is to bore wood out of the butt. So with the gun frame held tightly in a leather-faced vise, David started in with a brace and one-inch auger bit while I steadied and supported the stock. Attacking the grain end-on requires considerable force.

"You ever break out through the side?" I asked, watching David's face turn red as he leaned against the breastpiece.

"Not very often," he said, teeth clenched. "The apprentice usually gets harpooned when it happens."

"How so?"

"Because he's holding the stock and facing the bit. Just as you're doing."

"Then what?"

"You get a new apprentice and blame the old one for a botched-up job. Posthumously, of course."

After two bore holes, some gouge work inside, and mercifully no bloodletting, the gun balanced right on the money. "That's good for now," David said. "I'll take out a bit more later, after I've shaped up the head and put in the oval." He also would hand-cut two plugs from a scrap he'd earlier trimmed off the butt, matching the grain and fitting them to the bore holes so carefully that with the butt made off and checkered, they're impossible to find.

The stock is now fully shaped except for the head from the fences and frame back to a predetermined point behind the lockplates. This section he shapes with chisels, forming elegant curves by eye and touch, establishing crisp, graceful edges around the locks. Finally, time for more gunmaker's gothic.

Drop-points apparently evolved in the late seventeenth century, in flintlock days, as a decorative way of blending lockplates into the hand of a stock. They serve the same function now, and they've been standard fare for best-quality London guns since Joseph Manton's time. They test a stockmaker's mettle in several ways; their layout combines precise geometry and freehand drawing, while cutting them out is an exercise in chisel work where one slip can be a serious botch. The quality of his drop-points tells you quite a lot about a stockmaker's skill, and once you study them a bit, you can readily see the difference between truly superb points and good or even very good ones.

David spends about an hour and a half on each point, peers closely at them for a few moments, makes some minute changes. "I reckon a stockmaker generally works to the tolerance of a sixty-fourth," he says, "but there are two places that don't offer even that much latitude. Being off a sixty-fourth in the heading-up affects a gun's function over the long term; being off that much in a drop-point affects its appearance. They're equally important."

By this time, there's nothing at all in my gun's appearance to quarrel with, and more test-firing into the trap suggests its function will be equally good. And the fit? Perfect is no exaggeration. So long as I do my part and lift the gun right to my cheek, it points exactly where I look, no matter whether I mount it quickly or slowly, swinging left, right, up, down, or wherever. Which of course is what a fitted gun is supposed to do.

What started five days before as a nearly 4¼-pound blank now weighs a shade over a pound. With plugs and oval in place, it will weigh 17½ ounces, and the whole gun will scale six pounds, five ounces, a full quarter-pound less than it weighed with the old stock. If you could handle it blindfolded, you'd never guess it's a 12-bore gun with 29-inch barrels.

The blank yielded a leftover piece just the right size for a matching fore-end, but that's a job for another time. I'm booked on an afternoon flight out of Boston, and much as I'd like to, I cannot stay to watch David make and inlet a silver oval in the belly of the stock; sand it all down through successive stages, ending with a half-dozen de-whiskering treatments of oxalic acid and 600-grit paper; begin the long process of a London oil finish; lay out and cut the checkering at twenty-seven lines to the inch.

As I write this, at the end of September, the new stock's had its maiden voyage, for doves and snipe and blue grouse in Colorado. In a few days, we'll have a go at ruffed grouse and woodcock in Minnesota. Inconsistency usually is the most consistent part of my shooting, but I'm on a highly satisfying roll so far. It won't last, of course, but that won't be the gun's fault.

The wood is taking on a fine patina, thanks to about two dozen coats of linseed and a lot of rubbing. "Don't try to rush the finish," David said when I phoned him after it arrived. "It takes time to build up properly. Just keep rubbing it with your hands."

This is no hardship, because I can't keep my hands off it. Works of art affect me that way sometimes.

4

A Toast to the Trigger

If by happy chance you ever find yourself a guest at some function of the Worshipful Company of Gunmakers of the City of London, you'll hear the traditional gunmakers' toast, as elegant as a London gun: "To the trigger." And if your synapses aren't welded by the time the port gets slid around the table, you might wonder why the trigger. Why not drink to the barrels? Or the strikers? Or just to the gun?

Being an inquisitive sort, I once asked a kindly old gentleman who'd spent a lifetime in the London trade why gunmakers drink to the trigger. He peered at me over his glasses and smiled.

"Well, the trigger is the bit that sort of makes it all work, isn't it?"

True enough. It isn't worth much unless accompanied by lock, stock, and barrel, but as part of an integrated whole that includes the shooter as well as the gun, the trigger is a fulcrum where systems connect.

The process of shooting comprises two separate circuits, one neurological, the other mechanical, and both are logic circuits in that they function according to a predetermined sequence of events. Thus: A target appears. A series of electrical impulses between eyes and brain identify it as something to shoot and make certain judgments on its speed and angle. The brain, via more electrical language, directs the body to perform certain motions, culminating in a straightforward command to the trigger finger. This sets the mechanical process in motion. A pulled trigger disengages a sear. This releases stored energy from a spring, which sends a hammer falling against a firing pin, which crushes a priming chemical that detonates a spark into a quantity of powder, which ignites and burns and releases gas that drives a charge of shot down the barrel and into the air.

Assuming both sequences function as they should, the critical juncture clearly is the point where they interact, the point where the neurological process sets the mechanical process in motion—the point, in other words, where finger and trigger communicate. It's a point of transfer, of stimulus and response.

Ideally, this communication should be highly efficient, and it certainly can be. In actual practice it usually isn't—for one simple reason: The average trigger finger is a lot better at issuing a command than the average trigger is at carrying it out.

So while the gunmakers' toast is fine for the gunmakers, any shooter with an urge to knock back a few belts in honor of the gun would do well to slightly modify the toast and drink to the *good* trigger.

The good trigger deserves every tribute, celebration, paean, and praise. It has all the virtues of a Boy Scout and then some. It's clean and crisp, ready to do its job without the slightest hesitation, needs neither to be bullied nor babied, calls no undue attention to itself.

By comparison, the bad trigger is as loathsome a piece of work as ever besmirched an otherwise decent gun. It's the trigger you pull and then look to see if you didn't forget to take the safety off; the trigger that feels as if it's operating in a bed of gravel; the trigger that grates and creeps and grinds and drags its way through what seems an inch and a half of travel before the gun goes bang.

Sad to say, most of us, game shots especially, are far better acquainted with bad triggers than good ones because the average factory-made game gun comes spilling off an assembly line like a bottle of soda pop, virtually untouched by human hands.

Those hands are enormously important. By far the most common shortcoming among guns of moderate or even fairly high quality is a trigger-pull that's just too bloody hard. Machinery can create a mechanism without drag or creep, but only a pair of highly experienced hands wielding a stone can achieve a sweet, light, reliable let-off, and without that, neither gun nor shooter can function at their best.

If you've ever tried to take a shot with the safety still on, you have a good idea of what a hard trigger does to your shooting. It interrupts your swing, distracts your attention from the target, drags the muzzles down, and sends the shot low, if not behind as well. The lighter the gun, the more disruptive a heavy trigger.

Since handwork is considerably more expensive than machine work these days, you'll often see a correlation between the cost of a gun and the quality of its triggers. But not always. A few months ago, I tested an $8,000 Italian sidelock that had the creepiest triggers I've seen in years—triggers not nearly so good as those on a $2,500 boxlock by the same maker. I assume the sidelock was a fluke, but such things do happen.

Among factory pieces, the best triggers traditionally have come on target guns—from Remington's classic Model 32, through the ill-fated Model 3200, to the current crop of fine-quality trap, skeet, and clays guns by Perazzi and Beretta, Marocchi, Krieghoff, Ljutic, and others. The reason for this is simple: Serious target-shooters have always demanded good triggers and have been willing to pay for them, while hunters for the most part have simply accepted what the factories doled out.

This is not to suggest that the gunmaking industry is out to diddle poor Nimrod. It's always been a question of economics—give the customer what he wants at the lowest possible price and don't spend production money on anything he doesn't complain about. And now that product-liability suits have reached astronomical levels in both frequency and absurdity, not even mass complaining is likely to make any difference. Far more shooting accidents occur in the hunting fields than on target ranges, and any gun company with good sense is going to do everything possible to make it difficult for some dimbulb to shoot himself in the foot—even if it means turning out game guns with triggers so stiff they take both hands to pull. You can't blame the gun manufacturers for that.

The presumption, at least in the minds of judges and juries who don't know any better, is that a light trigger-pull is inherently dangerous. This is not true. A gun with a badly fitted sear is dangerous because a bump—or recoil from the first barrel—can set it off. But if sear and notch are in proper contact at the right angle and depth, the gun is highly unlikely to fire unless you pull the trigger—even if the necessary pressure is very little.

Which is not to say that the proverbial hair-trigger is desirable for anything but a target rifle. I know of world-class trap and skeet shooters who use triggers honed down to little more than a one-pound pull—acceptable on a target range, but entirely too light for hunting. Such a set-up may be perfectly safe against accidental knocks and jars, but it's not safe against a twig, a rowdy dog, nor a trigger finger desensitized by a glove or half-numb with cold.

By the traditional rule of thumb, optimum weight of trigger-pull is half the weight of the gun. In double guns, regardless of whether it has two triggers or only one, the first sear is set at one-half gun weight and the second at a half-pound more. There are several mechanical and behavioral reasons for this, one of which is to help prevent recoil from the first shot from jarring off the second sear.

In practical terms, the rule of thumb is not an absolute prescription. Naturally some latitude exists. My two favorite bird guns weigh in at 6¼ and 6½ pounds respectively, and each is set up for a 3½-pound pull on the front trigger and four pounds on the back one. My favorite target gun, on the other hand, is an eight-pound Marocchi Contrast over-under with a non-selective single trigger and three-pound pulls for both sears that are as sweet and chaste as a maiden's kiss. None of these guns exactly fits the rule, but each of them feels exactly right.

Feel, of course, is the whole point—or rather what you don't feel. To my thinking, trigger-pull should be matched to gun weight and also to the shooter, simply because some have larger, stronger hands than others. So the ideal weight is whatever offers just enough resistance to keep you from shooting too soon but not so much as to force you to shoot even a fraction too late. If you've never fired one, a gun with a trigger-pull of three to four pounds will be a revelation. You may be completely accustomed to the yank and strain of a heavy sear, but shoot two boxes of shells with a really good trigger and I guarantee you'll feel every excess ounce when you switch back.

I can also promise that switching back will be a temporary thing, because if shooting is important to you, you will forever after look upon a hard trigger as if it were something you just scraped off your boot.

The question, then, is what to do about it, and the first step is checking your favorite fowling piece to see if it's a candidate for improvement. For starters, cock it, put in a snap-cap or two, take off the safety and hang it on your trigger finger; any sear that'll support the entire weight of a gun is definitely too hard. If it won't, it still may be too hard, but you'll need a trigger-scale to find out just how stiff it is. Essentially, this is a modified version of the hang-type scale that fishermen use, graduated in ounces up to about five pounds. Any decent gun shop should have one and also have someone on staff who knows how to use it properly.

Although game guns come in quite a variety of gauges and weights, by far the majority of them weigh somewhere between 5½ and 7½ pounds, and in that category I'd say any trigger-pull over four pounds is too heavy. In the low end of the range—say less than six pounds—even a four-pound pull may be too much, though I personally consider three pounds the practical minimum for a field gun.

If you find your trigger could use adjustment, your options depend to some extent upon the gun itself. If you shoot a pump or autoloader you may be able to buy a whole new trigger group specially designed for target shooting. Several companies make these as aftermarket items for repeaters popular as target guns—Winchester Model 12, Remington 870 and 1100, and so on. Ads in the trap, skeet, and sporting clays magazines will give you a start toward finding them.

For trigger work on other guns, doubles and some repeaters, you'll need the services of a first-class gunsmith. If the maker is still in business you can inquire about having it done at the factory, but don't be surprised if the factory turns you down, and you should also be aware that some companies instantly void their warranties on new guns if you have them altered from factory specifications. You may thank our legal system on both counts.

Chances are your only choice is a gunsmith, and make no mistake—when I say "first-class" smith, I mean exactly that and nothing less. Trigger work is highly demanding; it requires a master's touch and plenty of experience, and it absolutely is not something you should trust to anyone but a master craftsman. Ask around for recommendations and references, and if you can't locate a top-notch independent, then inquire of such old-time, reputable shops as Griffin & Howe or Pachmayr.

Whoever you choose, ask up front if he's willing to guarantee the work—that is, guarantee that the trigger-pull will be crisp and clean, without creep or drag, will be within two or three ounces of the weight you specify, and most important, will stay that way. A badly fitted sear can change with just a bit of wear (so, for that matter, can a good one if the metal isn't properly rehardened), and for reasons I don't fully understand, it's as likely to get stiffer as it is to get lighter.

If he flatly refuses to make any guarantees, look elsewhere. But if he says he'll guarantee your trigger-pull to stay within reasonable limits, a couple of ounces or so, he's probably a man to trust because he knows that some wear is inevitable if you shoot a lot and also that ambient temperature, especially cold, causes slight, temporary change in triggers.

Don't expect first-quality work to come cheaply, any more than you'd insist on a bargain-basement price for having your appendix out or a hernia repaired. A good trigger man is as skillful as any surgeon, even if his fees aren't as high. Thirty dollars an hour is perfectly reasonable.

The gun first has to be stripped and thoroughly cleaned because dirt, hardened oil, and other gunk can interfere with its functioning, sears included. Actually adjusting the sears is entirely a matter of judgment and touch, typically done with a Carborundum stone, and the gunsmith has to reassemble the gun and check the sears with a pull-gauge after every stroke or two from the stone. He may have to repeat the process two or three times to get them just right.

Realistically, you should figure on spending at least $120 to have a double gun's sears adjusted. A repeater probably will cost less, but a single-trigger double may cost more because some require more time to disassemble and reassemble. In any case, you're clearly looking at something more than pocket change—although a lot less than you'd have to spend for a new gun. In fact, improving the triggers will make you think you have a new gun, one that you'll shoot better than ever before. That, my friend, is something well worth drinking to.

5

More About Triggers

A day or so after I mailed off the typescript for the chapter you just read, I was talking on the phone with an old friend who asked what I'd been working on lately. I told him I'd just finished a piece on triggers.

"Ah," he said, "I trust you told 'em that having two triggers on one gun is hopelessly old-fashioned."

We've had this discussion before, he and I, largely because he enjoys grousing about what he considers my reactionary taste in guns. You should hear him when I show up at the clays club or a dove-shoot carrying a hammer gun. I have a notion that when his mother told him to respect his elders, he thought she said "alders." At any rate, he spends a lot more time thrashing around among the one than he does practicing the other.

This time his ration of horse apples reminded me that I've had similar discussions with quite a few people, at least in abbreviated form. Someone will glance at one of my guns and say something like, "I don't know how you can shoot with those double triggers. I can't use 'em at all." I always ask why, partly because I'm interested to learn how different people relate to the gun, but also to find out if I'm about to hear one of the old wives' tales on triggers.

There are several, and they seem about equally divided between the categories of *Why Double Triggers Are Bad* and *Why Single Triggers Are Good.* The most common indictments have it that twin triggers are confusing, that they make a quick second shot more difficult, and that the way they're positioned creates two different lengths in the stock, one of which is either too short or too long. Single triggers, on the other hand, earn the praises of simplicity and speed, of being more amenable for shooting with gloves on, and of allowing stock length to be established once and for all.

None of these ideas is today's news. If you look through James V. Howe's classic 1934 opus *The Modern Gunsmith* you'll find the old master predicting, "there will come a time when all shotguns and double rifles will be equipped with single triggers" because among other reasons, "shifting from one trigger to the other changes positions of length" and with a single trigger, "the grip need not be relaxed, which is required on two triggers." The rest go at least as far back.

None is new, and by the same token none is true. Anyone who tells you he "can't" use double triggers is really saying that he's never had the chance or spent the time getting accustomed to them. Anyone with enough coordination to pick his nose or dial a telephone can get used to double triggers in fifty shots; all he has to do is spend one afternoon on a skeet field shooting doubles. In fact, if he really wants to get into the groove he can fire about fifty more shots and learn to reverse the sequence—pull the back trigger first and then shift to the front—without having to give it a thought. Using two triggers just isn't that tough.

The matter of a speedy second shot baffles me completely. After all, with two triggers you can use two fingers and fire both barrels at once. (It's no way to shoot skillfully, and double recoil can ring your chimes to a fare-thee-well, but at least it's possible.) Any single trigger that corks off two shots at once is badly in need of repair. Some of them are definitely quick, but you still have to release the trigger-blade between shots, and the mechanism still has to physically shift from one sear to the other. Saying that single triggers are quicker is like the old wheeze about autoloaders delivering faster second shots than pump guns. Not a chance. A self-loader is only as fast as its mechanism, but a pump is only as slow as the guy working the slide. A two-triggered double is faster than either one. (This whole argument of course begs the question on the difference between a fast second shot and an effective one, but old wives' tales seldom keep much company with practical reality.)

The stock-length question also makes little sense. I wouldn't presume to argue gunsmithing with James Howe—but I wouldn't want to take a shooting lesson from him either because his comments about changing position and relaxing grip tell me that he wasn't a shotgunner. Actually you can find similar statements elsewhere in print, either implying or stating flat out that you have to slide your hand backward on the grip to pull the rear trigger. I don't know where this got started, but if you shoot a two-triggered gun, you know better. If you've never fired one, take my word for it: You trip both triggers without moving anything except your finger.

Stock length is always measured from the front trigger, and the grip and guard-bow should be shaped so you can comfortably contact it with the pad of your finger, about halfway between the tip and the first joint—all without having your second finger jammed against the guard, where it will get smartly rapped from recoil. To fire both barrels you simply pull the front trigger, slide your finger over it and on to the back one. It's all one motion, nothing moves but your trigger finger, and none of it affects the way the stock feels in its length of pull.

For anyone inclined toward some detective work in tracking down the origin of all this, Howe's admonition about relaxing your grip on the gun is a good clue. A strong, controlling trigger-hand grip is a rifleman's approach, possibly a trapshooter's, certainly not a gameshot's. To someone who has no experience with a double-trigger gun, moving the hand between shots makes a certain sense, at least in theory, but all you have to do is try sliding your hand back and forth on the grip, as if playing a trombone the size of your nose, and try to imagine actually hitting a moving target at the same time.

Some shooters shy away from double triggers because their other guns have single triggers and they're afraid they wouldn't be able to switch back and forth. Not to worry. Once you get accustomed to both arrangements, you can interchange them with scarcely a thought.

You can, however, get yourself into a certain mindset—or at least I have. As best I remember, I haven't owned a side-by-side with a single trigger in about twenty years, and it's been almost thirty years since I had a two-trigger over-under. Since I use both types about equally often, my subconscious apparently has come to assume that any over-under I have in my hands has one trigger and that any side-by has two. I never realized this until a friend asked me to test a gun he'd just got back from the gunsmith—a nice little Fox 20-bore with a factory single trigger in the forward position.

The first field on our clays course is an incoming duck shot with simultaneous pairs dropping into a little pothole in front of the shooting stands. I got off one shot at the first pair, wondered why it wouldn't go bang the second time. I finally realized that I was pulling the trigger guard instead of a back trigger, but I did the same thing over again on the next two pairs. On the last two I was astonished at how much concentration it took to force myself into pulling the same trigger twice (and naturally missed the second target each time). It took about five more pairs before I could fire both shots without thinking about the trigger. I'm still bemused at how deep and selective certain grooves can become through time and repetition.

This is all a matter of mind, which is exactly where most shooters' difficulty with double triggers resides. The only people who truly can't use them are those with very small hands or very short fingers; for them, a single trigger obviously is the thing to have. For the rest of us it's purely a matter of preference, because one arrangement is not intrinsically better than the other.

I can see some good reasons to choose a single trigger for an over-under gun, because single triggers are especially well suited to half-hand and full-pistol stocks—which in turn are particularly appropriate to over-unders because they help keep both your hands on the same plane, just as a straight-hand stock does for a side-by-side. If the gun I had in mind offered the choice, I'd want my single trigger to be non-selective. This isn't to say that selective triggers can't be good. Some are excellent. But the selective capability has little or no practical value for a game-shooter, while its additional level of mechanical complexity invites malfunctions.

Moreover, there's no such thing as a truly fumble-proof selector—except for the various double-single designs that have cropped up over the past hundred years, made by Churchill in England, Brno in Czechoslovakia, Simson in Germany. Val Browning designed a double-single system that was standard fare in the Superposed until about 1939. Others have come out of Italy and Spain. At their most sophisticated, double-singles amount to two single triggers in one gun, each capable of tripping both sears. Firing sequence depends upon which trigger you pull. They're all clever pieces of engineering, but they're also as complicated as a Swiss watch, and bloody hell to put right when they go haywire. Any advantage they have over conventional double triggers is far more theoretical than real.

As for the garden-variety one-trigger systems, no one has yet come up with a selector that isn't to some extent either inconvenient, uncomfortable, or liable to hang up in mid-switch. Some are a lot better than others, but even at best they all require some deliberate attention—and anything that takes your mind off the target, however momentarily, does not promote good shooting. "Instant choke selection" has always been the great battle cry of selective-trigger marketing, but the only way to really accomplish that is to have a trigger for each barrel.

Which may be an old-fashioned concept, but it's one that shows no signs of dying out just yet.

LORE

6

Coming to Terms

Any gun book arguably is an exercise in preaching to the choir. Not that I intend to do much preaching, but given the notion that we're the choir it might be a good idea to be sure we're all singing from the same page, so to speak.

Like almost everything else, firearms have a lexicon all their own, a set of specialized words that denote various parts and functions. We don't, for instance, talk about "the long tubular things" on the front end of a gun; we simply use the word *barrels.*

Some gun terms are interesting in their own right, because they've been around long enough to undergo some evolution and accrue some history. Others are multiple words used to denote the same thing. Understanding these is especially important in talking about British guns and gunmaking—

and it's important to talk about that because the sporting gun as we know it literally is a British invention.

Some wag once observed that the Americans and the British are two peoples separated by a common language. And we are, at least to the extent that we often use different words for certain things. For instance, trousers that fasten just below the knee are a standard item of dress for shooting in England. We call them knickers; the British call them breeks. This seems innocent enough, but you'll draw some odd looks at an English shoot if you refer to your breeks, or anyone's, as knickers. To the British, knickers are ladies' underwear. You can imagine the spin this can put on a conversation.

Though British gun terms don't hold quite the same potential for embarrassment, there's plenty of opportunity for confusion because many of their terms are different from ours. Perhaps the most basic example is that when an Englishman uses the word *gun* he means "shotgun," not simply anything that shoots. The American military draws a similar distinction, or used to anyway, and if as a boot-camp grunt you made the mistake of using the word *gun,* you probably remember the pleasure of standing in front of your company reciting—and demonstrating—the little mnemonic couplet: "This is my rifle and this is my gun./This is for fighting and this is for fun." Useful stuff, sort of like knowing the difference between small arms and short arms.

Anyway, I like the British custom because it's specific, so from here on *gun* means shotgun and nothing else.

As for other general differences, at this point suffice it to say only that what we call screws are known in Britain by various names. Wood screws are screws, but machine screws are pins. Machine screws that act as pivots for other parts are typically called studs, sometimes pegs. In flint and caplock days machine screws were often called nails; this usage is nearly extinct nowadays, but some British gunsmiths still use the word once in a while.

For specific differences, to ensure that we're all speaking the same language, let's have a look at the various parts of a gun. For the sake of not insulting anyone I'm going to skip the gross anatomy and assume everyone knows what barrels, ribs, stocks, triggers, trigger guards, and that sort of thing are. For the sake of brevity I'll also stop short of identifying every last internal part. And for the same reason I'll use only one form of gun as the example, with the understanding that virtually all break-open guns—whether boxlock, sidelock, side-by-side or over-under—share most of the same parts and work on essentially the same principles.

One more point by way of preamble: the terms *action, frame,* and *receiver* are often used interchangeably, sometimes confusingly. For clarity I prefer to think of *action* as denoting the specific mechanism used to open a gun for loading—the hinge of a break-open gun or the sliding bolt of a repeater. In a repeater, the whole steel body is properly called the receiver since it receives loaded cartridges from the magazine and empties from the chamber.

For a break-action, however, *frame* seems to me the best word; it's the one part that all the main components touch, and besides, it doesn't receive anything. In the English trade the frame is commonly called the action, and the craftsman who specializes in shaping it, installing most of the parts, and fitting on the barrels is known as the actioner. My habit of distinguishing action and frame has prompted some ongoing debates with my English friends—with David Trevallion, for instance, the former Purdey man who made the stock from which these drawings were made. "If it's a bloody frame," he likes to argue, "then why don't we call the man who makes it a framer?" Maybe we should. After all, the English call the man who makes screws and pins the screwer; why not call him the pinner? It'd look better on his resume, anyway.

So to specifics...

Barrels and Fore-end

(1) We usually call this the *fore-end lug*. The British call it the fore-end loop. This is a carryover from muzzleloader and early breechloader days when barrels were fastened to stocks by flat steel bolts and fit crossways through the wood and into a rectangular hole in the lug—which therefore really was a loop.

(2) *Barrel flats*—so called, I suppose, because they're filed flat to fit closely with the upper surface of the action bar. This is the place to look for proof marks on a side-by-side gun.

(3) *Barrel lump*. In most best-quality guns half the lump is forged integrally with each barrel. These are called chopper lumps because separately they look something like a chopping tool. If you look closely you can find the seam, running lengthways down the center of the lump, where the two halves are joined.

In other cases the lump is a separate piece soldered or brazed between the barrels. We call this a dovetail lump; the English call it a dropper lump.

(4) The *hook*, so called because it hooks onto the cross-pin in the action bar to form the hinge. Together the hook and pin make up the joint, as the British call it; when the action wears to the point that it's loose, an English smith will say the gun needs rejointing.

In certain over-unders the hinge is designed on a somewhat different principle borrowed from cannonry. In old times cannons were nothing more than barrels resting on some sort of base. These barrels were cast or forged with heavy gudgeons, called trunnions, projecting from either side; these not only supported the barrel on its base but also allowed it to pivot up and down for changing elevation and trajectory.

Although trunnions would make a terribly awkward hinge for a side-by-side gun, the principle is ideal for an over-under. I don't know who first got the notion to use it, but that's how the first two great English over-unders—the Boss and the Woodward—are made. Italian gunmakers have since adopted it as virtually the standard over-under hinge.

This sort of joint simply combines rounded studs and corresponding notches, and it works equally well regardless of whether the studs are part of the barrels or part of the frame. Strictly speaking, trunnions are studs on the barrels, but since there's no other word that denotes studs on the frame, we can call it a trunnion hinge either way.

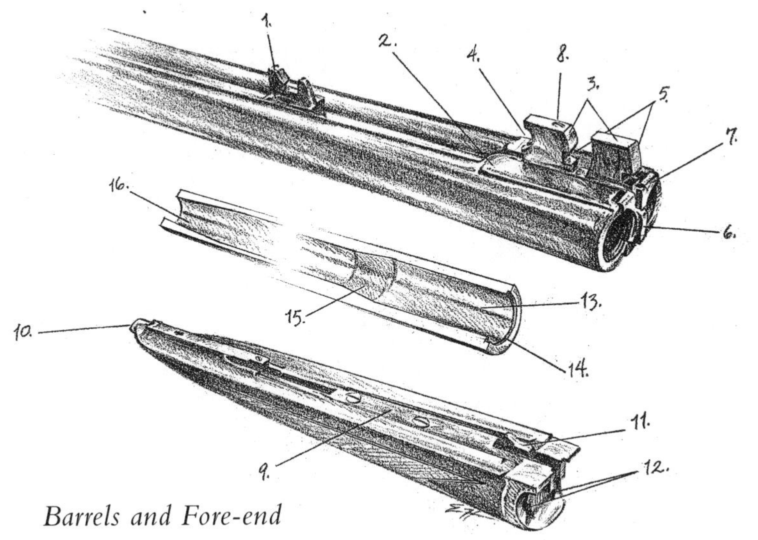

Barrels and Fore-end

(5) The *bites*—notches, in American terms—are where the fastening bolt fits to secure the action. There are lots of variations in fastening systems; the one you see here is the classic double-bite system patented by James Purdey the Younger in May 1863. It's been in almost universal use ever since the patent expired. English makers sometimes refer to fasteners as grips.

(6) Some guns, like this one, have a third fastener or third grip, sometimes called a *hidden* or *blind fastener*. If it were at the top of the barrels and fit into an open slot at the top of the frame, it would be called a rib-extension or doll's-head; it might or might not be engaged by a hook or cross-pin inside the frame.

(7) *Extractors* are sometimes called ejectors, though I prefer to think of ejectors as denoting the actual ejecting mechanism. In guns without ejectors these parts are made as one piece rather than two. English gunsmiths call them luggers, presumably because they lug cartridges out of the chambers. It's a charming term and technically a good one because it leaves no confusion over exactly what's being described.

(8) The *retaining screw*, or stop pin, allows the luggers to move freely back and forth but still keeps them attached to the gun.

(9) The entire metal body of the fore-end is called the *fore-end iron*. The curved rear section, which fits against the frame when the gun is assembled, is sometimes called the shoe.

(10) *Fore-end latch*. This one is the push-rod system invented by William Anson, who worked at Westley Richards in the latter nineteenth century and collaborated with John Deeley in inventing the boxlock gun. American makers, notably Fox and Parker, preferred the lever-type latch invented by John Deeley and James Edge, usually called the Deeley and Edge or simply the Deeley latch.

(11) *Ejector hammers*, or tumblers.

(12) *Ejector sears*—scears in British spelling. More about tumblers and sears when we get to the locks.

Although it's hard to see, the interior of a gunbarrel comprises some specific sections that have their own names. (13) *Chambers* belong entirely to breechloading guns, there to accommodate a self-contained cartridge. In order for the wadding, whether old-style felt and cardboard or the modern polyethylene versions, to create an effective gas-seal the interior diameter of the cartridge case needs to be almost identical to the interior diameter of the bore. Because its walls have to be of a certain thickness, the cartridge case's outside diameter is therefore larger than the bore—and so is the chamber.

In the old literature you'll sometimes come across references to so-called "chamberless" breechloaders. These were bored specifically for metal-cased cartridges, all-brass or zinc hulls that once were very popular. These typically have very thin walls, so the chambers didn't need to be much larger than the bores. The barrels weren't literally chamberless, but the differences in diameter usually were too slight to be readily apparent.

The chamber has to accommodate the flangelike rim of the cartridge, and this is done with a groove at the *breech-end* (14). It's usually called a rim cut. Some English 'smiths call it the rim space or head space, and the British Rules of Proof refer to it as the head recess or, more recently, simply the rim.

The tapered section between the front end of the chamber and the bore itself is the *forcing cone* (15). At the other end, just behind the muzzle, the *choke cone* (16) further reduces inside diameter from bore size to whatever degree of constriction the choke represents.

Action and Frame

(1) *Action bar.* The curved surface at the front end (2) is called the *knuckle*, derived I imagine from its similarity to a finger joint.

(3) *Cocking levers.* These extend back through the action bar and pivot upwards to cock the locks when the gun is opened.

(4) The *extractor toe*, which cams the luggers out as the barrels pivot on the hinge joint.

(5) The *cross-pin*, or hinge pin.

(6) The *bolt*. Combined with the bites in the barrel lump, this is the action's main fastener.

(7) The flat top surface of the action bar is called the action flats in England. We sometimes use the same term, but more

often we call this the *water table*—why, I don't know. An English friend suggested a possibility: When the action of a side-by-side gun is properly fitted the barrel flats and action flats don't actually touch, and the few-thousandths-inch gap between them is enough to collect and hold water on a rainy day.

This makes as much sense as any explanation I've heard, but I have a notion water table is one of those terms that will forever remain a mystery.

(8) The *standing breech*, also known as the breech face. Wear in the action creates a gap between the barrels and the breech face; the English say that such a gun is off the face.

The point where action bar and breech face meet at right angles is called the *break-off* (9). It's the point where the frame suffers the greatest stress when the gun is fired. To lend maximum strength, the break-off is always filed to a radius rather than a square corner. Even so, any gun that's mistreated to a steady diet of loads heavier than it was built for can eventually crack here. Then it becomes what's commonly known in the trade as a "junker."

The point where the top tang joins the frame is also called the break-off by some English craftsmen. This usage goes back to muzzleloader days, when barrels and breeches attached to the standing iron by breech-hooks while the iron itself was fastened to the stock by the top tang. The barrels, therefore, really did "break off" from the strap.

(10) We call these *firing pins*. To the British, they're strikers.

(11) This is the bolt that fastens the third grip. As I said before, not all guns have this extra fastener.

(12) Linguistically, the *fences* are among the most interesting parts of a gun, for the name goes back almost to the beginning of firearms. From wheellock to flintlock to caplock, the fence was literally that—a barrier behind the priming pan or the caplock nipple, meant to shield a shooter from bits of burning

powder or flying shards of a percussion cap. In those days fences came in all sizes and shapes.

With the advent of breechloaders the name was applied to the rounded bosses that seal the breeches. Their function is clear enough, but the terminology is sometimes arcane. British gunmakers—and by this I mean the craftsmen who actually build the guns—call them "the detonating." To these men a fence is a thin, raised ridge or bead that runs around the rear contour of the detonating and up over the top of the frame; it's there solely for aesthetics.

Shapes of fences and the ways they're carved make up a whole subgenre of terms. You may, for instance, hear of ball

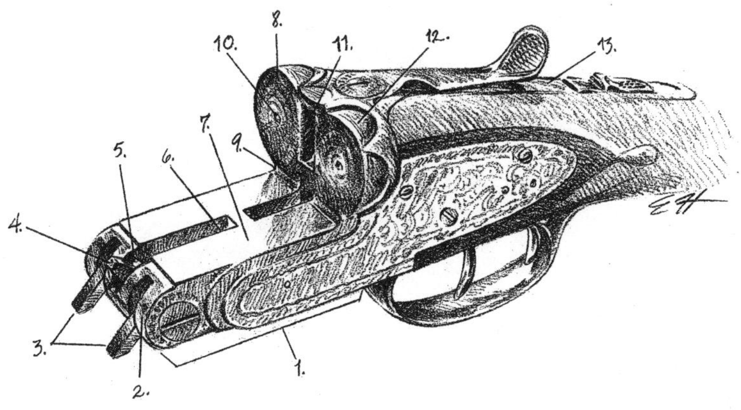

fences, which are round; or flat fences, which have a much shallower arc at the rear. The gun you see here is a good example of arcaded or umbrella fences, carved in a series of graceful arcs and points. Any English maker would do this upon request, but for a few—notably James Woodward and W. J. Jeffery—arcaded fences were something of a signature.

On some guns you'll see a little forward-pointing flange coming off the side of each fence. These are called side clips and they're meant for additional support against the lateral stress of firing heavy loads. British makers use them on pigeon and wildfowl guns. Lots of German and Austrian guns have them as well, mainly because Teutonic makers seem to think there's no such thing as too many fasteners or action supports.

When side clips are very closely fitted, as they are in a top-quality gun, the edges can be almost as sharp as knife blades, and they can do a remarkably good job of slicing your fingers if you aren't careful.

(13) *Top tang*, or in England, top strap. There's also a bottom tang or strap, mostly hidden by the trigger guard. In classic English and older American guns the straps are what hold the frame and the stock together. The stock is fastened on by two pins. The main one, called the breech pin, goes in from the top, underneath the top lever, and screws into a part of the trigger plate known as the trigger box. The rear pin goes in from the bottom strap to the rear end of the top strap, just behind the safety button—or thumb-piece, as the English say. This one is called the hand pin because the British call this part of the stock the hand.

Stock

(1) The *head* of a gunstock comprises the complex set of surfaces where the wood actually touches the frame. Fitting this is called heading-up, and functionally it is the most critical aspect of stockmaking because the long-term welfare of the finished gun depends upon a good marriage at this point. In a sidelock gun the process involves about thirty-seven-zillion bearing surfaces in more dimensions than are known to science, and for a best-quality job, every one is fitted to less than the thickness of a layer of smoke. Watching a first-class stocker perform the job lends clear meaning to the words "patience" and "precision."

The stock head ends with the *drop points* (2). These are purely decorative—or as David Trevallion calls it, gunmaker's gothic. They're there because tradition says they should be, and they take an ungodly amount of time and skill to shape. Look at enough stocks and you'll soon begin to see that not all drop points are created equal. Perfect points are to my mind one of

the signs of consummate craftsmanship.
(3) What we call the *grip* of the stock is the hand to a British gunner, both of which make sense because it's where a shooter's trigger-hand grips the gun. We also call it the wrist. The typical forms are straight, half, and full-pistol. In addition to these, English stockers use other standard forms such as the quarter-hand, Prince of Wales, and George V grips.

A diamond hand is a grip that's not rounded on the sides but rather shows a distinct edge leading backward from the rear of the lock, through the drop point. If you sawed the stock in half at the hand and looked at it end-on you'd see a diamond shape rather than an oval. It's wonderfully comfortable to hold. Not many American makers used it, but lots of English makers did. At present Holland & Holland seems to use the diamond hand more than any other maker.

In the British trade the *thumb hole* (4) is where the *comb* (5) rises up from the hand. In a custom-made stock it will be set back just the right distance to comfortably accommodate the fleshy base of your thumb as you hold the gun.

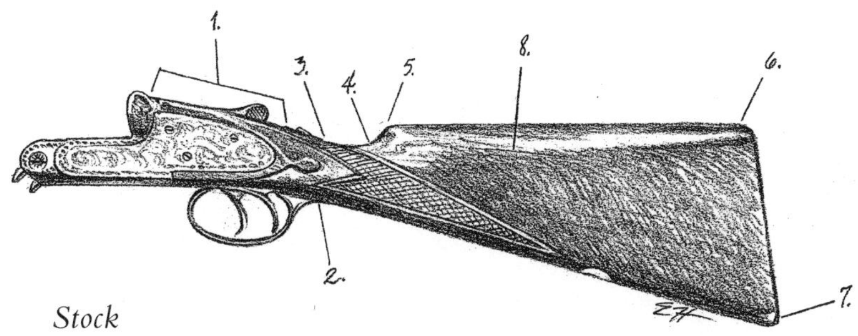

Stock

The drop of a stock, which the English call the *bend*, is measured at the comb and the heel (6). The English call the heel the bump; to them the heel is the entire rear surface, what we call the butt. A buttplate in the U.S. is therefore a heelplate in the U.K. We all agree, however, that the *toe* (7) is the toe. In prescribing dimensions for a custom fit, some makers specify a measurement at the *face* (8), where the stock actually touches the shooter's cheek.

Locks

To my thinking, a best-quality gunlock is the loveliest bit of machinery ever made, precise as a Swiss watch, elegant in its simplicity. Naturally, designs vary from one lockmaker to another. Some use coil springs. And some, such as the Beesley-patent lock that Purdey has used for more than a hundred years, are unlike any other. What you see here is a good example of a classic English sideplate lock.

Because the *mainspring* (1) is situated in front of the works and fits into the action bar, this is a bar-action lock—barlock, for short. If the spring were located behind the works it would be a back-action or backlock. Backlocks are the older form and now are more commonly used in rifles than in guns.

Either way, the parts are the same. The *tumbler*, or hammer (2), is the main moving piece. Its *axis* (3) extends through the lockplate, and its outer end is typically filed with a raised bar, engraved with an arrow or inlaid with a thin band of gold to serve as an indicator of whether the lock is cocked or tripped. A raised shoulder on the lockplate, called the *anvil* (4), supports the fixed limb of the mainspring and acts as a stop for the tumbler.

Tumbler and mainspring are connected by the *swivel* (5), sometimes called the connector. (In the inset drawing, the mainspring is disconnected for a better view of the swivel.) Originally, the working limb of the spring bore directly on the tumbler, but in the early 1770s some English lockmaker devised the swivel as a means of reducing friction and improving mechanical efficiency. Swivels have been part of gunlocks ever since.

At the rear of the tumbler is the *sear notch* (6), which the English call the bent. The *sear* (7) holds the tumbler in the cocked position until a pull of the trigger—which British makers sometimes call the tricker—lifts the sear nose out of the bent. The *sear spring* (8) keeps the sear in position to drop into the bent when the lock is recocked.

Like all best-quality locks, this one is fitted with an *interceptor* (9), also called the safety sear. The lock is designed so that the trigger lifts both the main sear and safety sear at the same time, but if the main sear is jarred out of its bent by something other than a pull on the trigger—if the gun is dropped, for instance—the interceptor catches the tumbler and prevents it from hitting the striker.

The interceptor has its own spring (10) to keep it in proper position.

It isn't exactly a working part, but the *bridle* (11) is a key component because it supports the tumbler in such a way

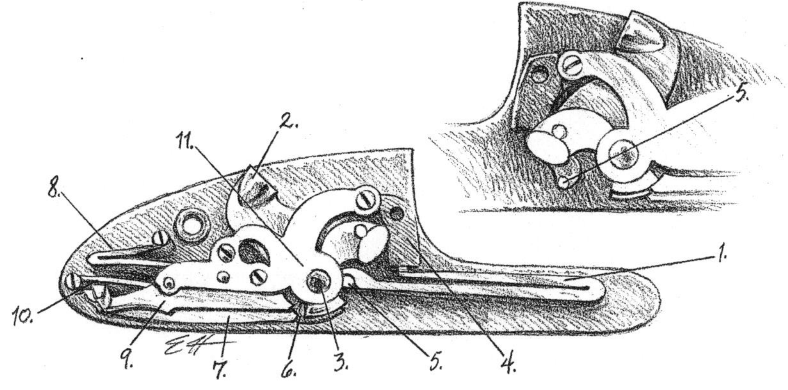

Locks

that allows it to pivot with minimum friction. Its invention, sometime in the seventeenth century, was an important milestone in the evolution of the gunlock.

Bridles come in a vast variety of shapes, some simple, others highly complex. It's the one part that allows the lockmaker much opportunity to show off his aesthetic sense as well as his skill. The comma-shaped hole in this bridle serves no purpose other than demonstrating that the man who made it was a master filer. More gunmaker's gothic—and this bridle is simple compared with some others.

Once in a while you'll come across a set of locks with gold-plated parts. I suppose this has occasionally been done for decoration, but the main reason is that gold doesn't rust or corrode—and corrosion was a particular concern for guns and rifles meant to be used in tropical climates, as a lot of them were during the great age of British colonialism.

The inner sides of the lockplates sometimes are engine-turned, or jeweled, for decoration. Typically, all the lock parts are polished bright after being hardened, but a few makers leave their bridles case-colored. It's an exceptionally handsome effect.

On some guns you'll notice a tiny lever on the outside of one lockplate, usually the left. It actually is the head of the pin that holds the locks in place, and it's made that way so you can remove the pin without using a screwdriver and dismount the locks.

The hand-detachable system made this way was a Holland & Holland invention. Other makers, both British and German, came up with different means of accomplishing the same thing. The key lock is one; each lockplate has a little keyhole, and the gun came supplied with tiny, skeleton-type keys for turning camlike fasteners inside. Key locks are uncommon, but you come across them now and then. Finding a gun that still has the keys with it is more uncommon yet.

As a variation on the Holland & Holland system, some makers hinge little round plates to their pins. These fold down into recesses in the plates and fit flush with the surface. They're almost invisible except for a tiny, crescent-shaped gap that allows you to raise the plate with a fingernail. The drawback is that it doesn't take much dust or corrosion to make the hinge sticky, which usually means a broken fingernail and then a scratched plate from the knife blade or other tool you have to use to pry up the finger-piece. Of all the various systems, the Holland & Holland lever is still the best.

The hand-detachable concept was applied to boxlocks in at least one notable instance—the famous Westley Richards droplock, patented in 1897. The bottom of the frame is actually a trap-door held shut by a spring-loaded latch. Remove the plate and the main lock parts—tumbler, sear, and mainspring, all fastened together as a unit—simply drop out of slots in the action bar. It's a brilliant piece of engineering.

Hand-detachable locks are a mixed blessing. Being able to readily pull them off is sometimes truly useful, but it's also a temptation for just fiddling with them—especially for people who shouldn't be.

But I promised not to do much preaching, and that last sentence has all the earmarks of a sermon about to begin. So it's time to move on.

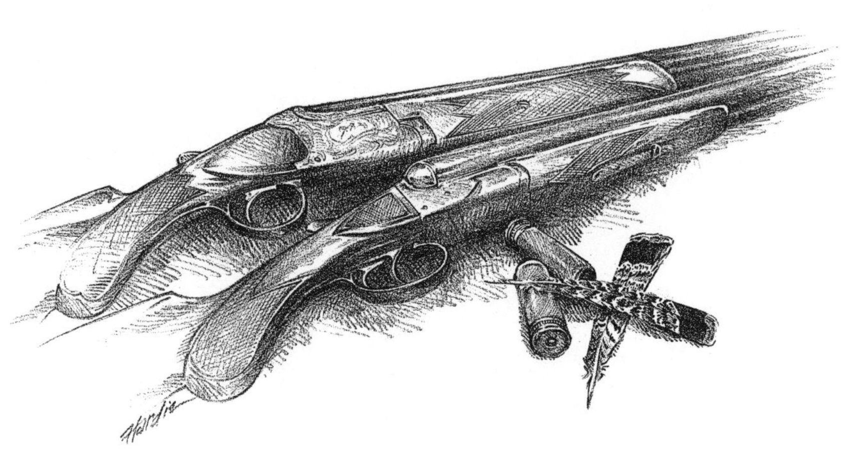

7

Over-Under or Side-by-Side

Gunning, like nearly everything else worth doing, has its ongoing debates. Is 16-gauge better than 20? One trigger better than two? Long barrels better than short? This better than that? On and on.

Although we seem to be living in a particularly contentious age, polemics are nothing new to the gunning world. Shooters and gunmakers alike have at various times argued the relative merits of flintlock versus caplock, breechloader versus muzzleloader, black powder over smokeless, twist barrels over steel. Through the greater part of this century, the most durable debate has centered on whether the over-under is better than the side-by-side, and vice versa. Somewhere in my files is a folder, half an inch thick, of magazine articles devoted to just that question. Some go back sixty years or more and, if nothing else, prove that no approach is so oblique, no detail so arcane, and no reasoning so outrageous that someone hasn't already thought of it.

The question of whether one is "better" than the other is fun to kick around with friends. It's a harmless opportunity to parade our preferences and prejudices, construct ingenious—and sometimes ingenuous—arguments and torture logic into bizarre convolutions. At the very least it keeps us occupied and out of trouble.

It isn't very instructive, though, since "better" and "best" are largely meaningless unless we qualify them half to death. In either case, taking that approach obscures a truly intriguing question: How can two essentially similar guns be so different?

And different they are, although not, it seems to me, for the reasons you hear most often. Some have argued that one or the other is inherently stronger (not true), inherently better balanced (also not true), and more accurate (definitely not true). The most common note, twanged time and again by those who tout the superiority of the over-under, is the fabled "single sighting plane."

For a long time, I had a feeling the idea originated with John Browning. Of course, Browning didn't invent the phrase, any more than he invented the over-under gun. "Single sighting plane" appears in the literature well before Browning came up with the Superposed. There's no question that he helped make it a cliché of American gun lore.

Certainly it was Browning who brought the over-under into the modern age, and Browning who made a point of describing its advantage by using a yardstick as a metaphor. One could, he argued, more accurately sight down the narrow edge than down the broad dimension.

Now on the surface that may seem like common sense. But think about it for a moment and the whole thing collapses into nonsense. No gun has more than one "sighting plane," no matter how many barrels it has or how they're arranged. More important, "sighting" has no more to do with shotgun shooting than it does with canals on Mars. Try to hit a moving target by sighting along a gunbarrel, and you might as well save a cartridge. You need to watch the target, not the barrel. If the gun fits and if you mount it properly the barrels will point where you look. If it doesn't fit or if you mishandle it, they won't. It's as simple as that.

Putting both myth and aesthetics aside, the most significant difference between an over-under and a side-by-side, to me at least, is a matter of feel. They have all the same parts and work the same way, but they don't feel the same. Over-unders don't feel much different from pumps or autoloaders, but side-by-sides feel different from all of them. This I find curious, indeed.

Sighting, as we use the term in rifle shooting, certainly doesn't apply, but rifle shooting itself offers a clue. We are, in a very real sense, a nation of riflemen. From colonial days until scarcely a generation ago we depended upon the rifle to tame a wilderness and defend the civilization that came after. Our gunning tradition, by comparison, is a mere sprout, and in general we tend to handle guns as if they were rifles, first snugging them to the shoulder and cheek and then swinging on the target. This is true whether we're shooting American-style trap or skeet, where the rules allow a deliberate gun-mount before calling for the target, or whether we're shooting game. Watch your friends sometime; more often than not, you'll see the gunbutts hit their shoulders before the muzzles start tracking the birds.

The English, whose shooting traditions are far older than ours and distinctly geared more toward the gun than the rifle, take a different approach. They move the muzzles first, and essentially start the swing while raising the gun. A British or British-taught shooter won't bring the gun to his shoulder until the barrels are on the flight line and ahead of the target, and he'll pull the trigger at almost the same instant the butt touches his shoulder and cheek.

This isn't to argue that either technique is right or wrong (although the English style seems to me more consistent and more readily adaptable to targets at various and unexpected angles), but it does help explain some of the handling differences between the over-under and the side-by-side.

The over-under feels like a rifle: that is, you can mount it, snuggle up to the stock, and everything seems comfortable. Not so the side-by-side, or not so for me, anyway. I cannot comfortably shoot a side-by from the high-gun position, not even guns tailored to my stock prescription. It's not a matter of recoil, either. It just doesn't feel right, even before I pull the trigger. I shoot a side-by-side far better, no matter what the target, if I'm not locked into the gun to start with—if, in other words, I shoot it by the British technique. Then everything seems to work as it should.

The over-under, on the other hand, seems a bit more technique-adaptable, and I can shoot one about equally well (or equally poor, as the case may be) from either the high- or low-gun position. The same is true of repeaters. They all feel, to a great extent, like rifles, and are therefore amenable to being handled like rifles. When I first realized the difference I thought it was some peculiar quirk of my own. But I've since asked a lot of other shooters about it, shooters well experienced with both over-unders and side-by-sides, and most tell me they've noticed the same thing. As one put it: "I always shoot better at game with a side-by-side and better at targets with an over-under. I dunno why."

Well, I dunno why, either. Not exactly, anyway. I suspect it has much to do with the relative positioning between the hands and eyes. A proper side-by-side puts both ends of the gun in your hands at about the same level, and that level is somewhat higher, relative to your eyes, than you get with an over-under. You can test this yourself. Hold a side-by-side and you'll notice that both barrels lie deep within the cup of your forward hand and that the rib, which delineates the horizontal plane your eye should follow toward the target, is scarcely more than an inch above your palm. If it's properly stocked there shouldn't be much bend at the wrist, so your trigger hand is similarly high up in relation to the rib.

Now switch to an over-under. The rib will be at least twice as far above the palm of your leading hand, and your trigger hand will be proportionately farther below the top of the standing breech, where your sight-line begins. Finally, pick up a rifle and see which of the two guns its feel most resembles.

Clearly the over-under and side-by-side require some subtle but significant difference in handling. A side-by-side forces you to bring the gun up to your face, which is what the English insist you should do anyway. They invented the side-by-side game gun, after all, so I'm inclined to take their word for the most effective way of using it. Experience seems to bear it out.

Considering its riflelike handling character it's not hard to see why so many Americans prefer the over-under and why so many of us shoot it well. Nor, by the same token, is it hard to understand why some are inclined to flatly argue that it's the better of the two. I don't know about that, but I do know they're different enough to warrant some serious study. Consequently, I intend to shoot as many specimens of both as I can get my hands on, and keep at it until I figure it out. It could take years...with any luck at all.

8

Who Killed Sweet Sixteen?

Once she was belle of the ball, the queen of two continents. She was ageless, a paragon of grace. Now, like an old photograph so faded that only the frame remains, she is little more than a memory of the days when she was truly sweet sixteen.

Gervase Markham probably was the first man in history to advocate any particular shotgun gauge in print (in his book *Hunger's Prevention, or The Whole Art of Fowling by Water and Land*, published in London in 1621). Since wingshooting would not be introduced to England for another forty years, Markham predictably centers his discussions on taking feathered game with nets, snares, birdlime, and such, but he does mention that the wildfowler could find good use for a six-foot fowling piece with a bore slightly smaller than that of the military arquebus, or about two-thirds of an inch.

That's 16-gauge.

The 16 was one of only a handful of gauges, defined by the English Gun Barrel Proof Act of 1868, that survived into the age of the breech-loading gun. The British never liked it to any great extent, but elsewhere in Europe the 16-gauge was predominant for nearly a hundred years. Before they began turning out guns meant specifically for the American market, Belgian, French, and German makers built more 16s than all other gauges combined.

In America, from the turn of the century into the 1950s, the 16-gauge was the uplander's darling. For many years the standard European 65 mm (2⁹⁄₁₆-inch) case was also the American standard, and the ounce of shot it held was all a quail or grouse or woodcock hunter needed. The 2¾-inch version, developed during the 1920s, will hold ⅛-ounce more shot and a bit more powder, which made the 16 no slouch in a duck blind. Ballistically, the 16-gauge can do almost anything a 12-bore can, and it does everything better than a 20.

Still, it's hardly a secret that sweet sixteen is headed for the sunset. Gun writers have been turning out obituaries and eulogies for twenty years or more. One by one, gunmakers have quit building them.

So who killed sweet sixteen?

Economics did. And technology did. So did the whims of fashion. But of all the factors that have contributed to the 16's demise, none really have anything to do with the intrinsic merits of either the cartridge or the gun.

Before World War II, most shotguns were built on frames of a size and weight proportionate to the size of their barrels. Parker carried the notion further than anyone else, and Fox built 16s and 20s on the same frame, but all of the great American doubles were otherwise built on at least three different frames—12, 16, and 20. Some repeaters also had similarly scaled receivers—the Remington Model 31 and the Winchester Model 12, for instance. So far as I know, the Browning Sweet Sixteen, made from 1937 to 1976, is the only autoloader ever built on a true 16-gauge receiver.

The Winchester 21 is the last true 16-gauge double built in America. By the late 1970s, orders for them amounted to only about four guns per year. There are even fewer now.

Made up on a proper frame, a 16-gauge double is something very like the perfect gun. It has neither the bulk of a 12-gauge nor the reedy profile of a 20. It can be a pound or more lighter than an equivalent 12 and yet outweigh a similar 20 by only a few ounces. Its handling is dynamic without being whippy, and it is substantial enough to comfortably dampen recoil. A fine 16 can steal any bird shooter's heart.

Unfortunately, few of the 16s built after the war share such qualities. Post-war economics dictated that gunmakers simply could no longer afford to use a different frame for every gauge. Most finally settled on two, large and small, 12 and 20. The 16 ended up a bastard child, 16-bore barrels on a 12-gauge frame. All its advantages in weight, in grace and dynamics, were gone. Shooters decided, rightly enough, that if they had to accept a gun that weighed as much as a 12-bore, it might as well be a 12-bore. Moreover, the Ithaca Model 37 Featherlight had in 1937 demonstrated that 12-gauge guns could be built to 20-gauge weights and still be both durable and reasonably comfortable to shoot. In the 1950s and '60s, the growing use of lightweight alloys in gunmaking pushed the 16 even farther out of the mainstream.

That there is no real place for the 16 in target shooting hasn't helped either. A 16-bore is fine at sixteen-yard trap, but beyond that, trapshooting is a 12-gauge game. A skeet field is an excellent showplace for the 16's handling qualities, and in fact, the first national skeet-shooting championship was won with a 16. But there is no 16-gauge event in either American or International skeet. Nothing in the rules says you can't use one—but only in the 12-gauge or any-gauge events. You'll look a long time before you find a 16 at any target club these days.

Ironically, what really kept the 16 out of skeet shooting is that it so nearly duplicates the ballistics of a 12-gauge target load. Damned if it did and damned if it didn't.

The tides of fashion, too, have run against it, unfairly

perhaps and certainly without much basis in practical fact, but certainly with telling result. In the fifteen years after World War II, the American affinity for believing that more is better prompted a great interest in the 12-gauge. No doubt influenced by his wartime indoctrination in the virtues of sheer firepower, the average sportsman of the 1950s seemed to feel that only a wimp would shoot anything smaller than a 12-bore or want a gun that held fewer than a pocketful of shells. The 16, once regarded as the seasoned bird shooter's ideal, was relegated to a status somewhere between an old man's gun and a toy.

When that particular wave of nonsense began to peter out in the early 1960s, the fad swung the other way. Twelve-gauges were for meat-hunters and game hogs. If you were a real sport, you had a 20. Arms and ammunition manufacturers joined a brigade of sporting journalists on the 20-gauge bandwagon and convinced the shooting public that the path to paradise was .615 inches in diameter. By then, the 16 had been kicked so far out of the picture that it hadn't a chance.

A few die-hards clamored for someone to bring back a three-inch cartridge for the 16, claiming that it would rescue the ailing lady from the brink. Fortunately, no one did. Better that she die with dignity.

And die she will. Five or ten years from now, you'll be hard-pressed to find a new production 16 anywhere in the world.

Still, there's a bright side. Many thousands of fine old doubles were built in 16-gauge, and they are the last real bargains to be had. Don't expect to find a mint-condition, high-grade 16 for sale at a cut-rate price; collector-quality guns will always bring collector-quality prices. But if you'd be happy having a fine old gun to fondle and shoot, one that shows enough use to disqualify it as a prime collector's piece, then a 16 might be just the ticket.

Prices for noncollector 16s have been depressed for years. Among the classic American doubles, 16s these days often are priced 10 to 20 percent lower than 12-bores of the same grade and condition. Some will fetch only half as much as similar 20s.

Finding ammunition is sometimes a problem even now, and the situation isn't likely to improve. Factory shells will be available for a good long time, but any serious 16-gauge shooter would do well to take up handloading.

If you've never done it, a good day's quail or grouse shooting with a trim old 16 is a day you won't soon forget. Then you'll know why sweet sixteen's remaining beaux usually are silvery old-timers who seem to know something that most others don't. Ours may be the last generation to know her as anything other than a curiosity. Which is why shooting with my 16s sometimes feels like dancing with a ghost.

9

Twenty-Eight to the Pound

"The small-bore gun is not the toy some suppose it to be."
W. W. Greener

"Actually, there isn't much excuse for it."
Jack O'Connor

It was clear by 1880 that small-bore breechloaders could be effective game guns. The London Gun Trials of 1875 and 1879 had proven that a well-made 20-bore in the hands of a competent shot could more than hold its own against larger guns inside forty yards, and subsequent experience proved that even smaller gauges could deliver some surprising results. Greener, with a mixture of pride and bemusement, reported that an eleven-year-old boy set the London shooting circles abuzz by killing as many as thirty-eight of fifty best Blue Rock pigeons at twenty-seven yards rise with a 28-bore. Greener's pride came from the fact that he'd built the gun, his bemusement from the almost universal belief that really small guns aren't supposed to shoot that well. Another London gunner reported similar results at game, writing to Greener in 1885, "I can only say your 28-bore gun cannot be improved upon."

Many shooters who had never tried a 28-bore scoffed. Many still do. And the 28-gauge still has its surprises.

It was a relative latecomer to America and caused no great stir when it did arrive. The 28-gauge had so little impact upon American gunning that most of the great makers ignored it altogether or waited until skeet shooting finally created a market, almost a generation after the first American 28s were built. Neither A.H. Fox, L.C. Smith, Lefever, nor Baker ever put a 28-gauge into production.

Parker made the first American 28-gauge doubles about 1905. Around the same time, Remington chambered its Rider single-barrel in 28-bore, but the greater share of the small-bore market, which in those days was every bit as brisk as a tombstone, went to the double.

Parker's first serious competition came from Ithaca, which first offered the 28-gauge in 1911 as a chambering for its then-current Flues Model double. When the New Ithaca Double was put into production in 1925, it, too, was made as a 28.

Harrington & Richardson built some single-barrel hammer guns in 28-gauge during the 1910s and '20s, but the rest of the arms industry made no effort to adopt the little cartridge until the 1930s, when skeet shooting blossomed. There, the 28 finally found a home.

By then the double gun was in deep doldrums, and most of the 28-gauges built in America over the next fifty years would be repeaters. Winchester brought out a 28-gauge version of the Model 12 in November 1934—probably the first such repeater built anywhere in the world and certainly the first made to 28-gauge scale. The earliest guns could be had with a 26- or 28-inch barrel, either plain or solid-ribbed, and they weighed about 6¼ pounds. Ventilated ribs came available shortly after. The Model 12 ultimately was made in fifteen different styles of 28-gauge field and skeet guns, a dozen of which were discontinued in 1945, two more in 1955, and the last in 1959.

In 1936 Winchester offered the Model 21 in 28-gauge

as a special-order item. Like the .410s that came along nearly twenty years later, the 28-gauge Model 21s were built on 20-gauge frames. Iver Johnson chambered its Skeeter side-by-side in 28-bore during the 1930s. If you had the money, you could have a 28 built by Beretta, Francotte, Merkel, or any of the British makers. Still, the 28's niche in the American market remained a tiny one.

Shooting sports of all kinds enjoyed something of a renaissance following World War II, and a new vitality rippled through the arms-making industry. Even though the general trend favored big-bore guns and lots of firepower, the 28-gauge got a share of attention both as a skeet and game gun. In 1952 Remington brought out the first 28-gauge autoloader, a scaled-down Model 11-48. Both Parker and Ithaca doubles were out of production for good, and if you wanted a new 28-bore double, it had to be either a Model 21 Winchester or an import.

The 28 fared better in the 1960s than it ever had, at least in the variety of available guns. Browning introduced the 28-gauge Superposed in 1960, and before the decade was over, 28s were available as over-unders from Charles Daly, Krieghoff, SKB-Ithaca, and Winchester—all but the Krieghoff were built in Japan, and none were built on true 28-gauge frames. You could get side-by-sides from Webley & Scott, Beretta, Darne, and Franchi, inexpensive single-barrels from Winchester and Stevens. High Standard introduced a 28-gauge pump in 1966. Remington adapted both its Model 870 pump gun and its Model 1100 autoloader to 28-gauge in 1969.

Today the picture is brighter still. The Remington 1100 and 870 are the only 28-gauge guns currently made in America, but both Winchester and Browning offer Japanese-built over-unders. Winchester's Model 23 side-by-side, also made in Japan, is now available in a Classic series as two-barrel sets—12 and 20, 28 and .410. The remarkable Parker Reproduction, yet another Japanese item, is the old Parker brought back to life. The 28-gauge, on the market now for a year, is built on the old standard No. 00 frame. On the import market, you can get a 28 from any of almost two dozen European makers. Most are side-by-sides. Beretta makes a production over-under in 28-bore, and you can bespeak a custom gun from England or Italy if you're feeling flush. Costs of the imports range from cheap to serious, and so does quality.

Still, not all that many 28-gauge guns are actually built. The skeet world, which comprises the majority of 28-gauge shooters, has largely abandoned the notion of separate guns for each event. Most serious skeeters nowadays use either multi-barrel sets—20, 28, and .410 barrels on 12-gauge frames—or interchangeable barrel tubes for the small gauges. To shoot the small-bore events, you simply slide the proper set of tubes into your 12-gauge gun and have at it.

Tubes certainly are an economical alternative—a full set from Briley or Kolar for $1,000 or less versus four guns from Perazzi or Marocchi or Shotguns of Ulm at about $2,000 apiece. And you can't buy them anyway, because none of the best-quality target guns are available as small-bores built to scale. So if you want to compete seriously in all skeet events, you shoot small-bores that weigh more than 12-gauges. Tubes are a poor compromise for anyone who takes delight in the handling qualities of the various gauges, but they work.

Twenty-eight-gauge specimens of the great American doubles are collectors' darlings. No maker built very many of them. The rarest of all is L.C. Smith—or rather *the* L.C. Smith, because there was only one, an 00 Grade Hunter Arms gun, serial number 100. It probably was built around 1910. At last report, the Hunter family still owned it.

The factory records no longer exist, but Winchester estimates that no more than 200 Model 21 production guns were built as 28-bores. Even on 20-gauge frames, they're nifty little things, and hindsight still nettles me for turning down the one I could have bought for $2,000 fifteen years ago.

Ithaca built more 28s than any other American maker. No record remains of how many Flues Models there were, but records do exist for the New Ithaca Double (NID) series. Between 1925, when the NID was introduced, and 1948, when it went out of production, Ithaca built a total 415 28-bores: 295 of them Field Grade, forty-two in No. 1, fifty-eight in No. 2, five No. 3s, ten No. 4s, three in No. 5, and two No. 7s. Curiously, more than twice as many NIDs were made as .410s than as 28s.

Not surprisingly, Parkers are the most sought-after and fetch the highest prices. In terms of gauge alone, only Magnum 10-bore, 8-bore, 24-gauge, and .410s are rarer. The most famous of the Parker 28s probably is the A-1 Special that somehow came to be called the Little Persuader (which gets my vote as the silliest name ever given a shotgun); it's the gun that brought $95,000 at a Christie's auction in 1981. It has sold two or three times since, and you can bet the price hasn't gone down. Less well known is the DHE 28-gauge that Carole Lombard ordered in 1936 as a gift for Clark Gable. It's still in virtually mint condition and, except for the initials CG, is a typical Remington Parker—but those initials lend it a human connection more interesting than any price tag.

Besides being eminently collectible, the old 28-bores can be great fun to shoot. But choose wisely if you decide to do that, for several reasons. In any reasonable condition, a 28-gauge Parker or Ithaca is likely to bring a premium price, and though further use of a gun that's already been well used won't necessarily lower the value, it won't raise it either. The question of use is best answered gun by gun in terms of originality and condition.

Age, too, is a consideration, because in the old days the standard 28-gauge cartridge was 2½ inches long, and the earliest guns were so chambered. The original load was 1¾ drams of black powder, or its equivalent in smokeless, and ⅝-ounce of shot. Sometime after World War I, ammunition makers developed a 2⅞-inch case that held a bit more powder and ¾-ounce of shot. The now-standard 2¾-inch cartridges came along in the 1930s as skeet loads; they also held ¾-ounce of shot. Shells of all three lengths were readily available until World War II.

Ithaca began boring all its 28-gauge chambers to 2⅞

inches in September 1931. Parker did the same thing, but I don't know exactly when. All 28-gauge Model 12s have 2⅞-inch chambers, but some of the Model 21s built before World War II are bored 2½ inches. It's wise to have any older 28 miked out by a gunsmith.

If you've never shot a 28-gauge, you're in for a treat, provided you don't ask more of it than it's capable of doing. Unfortunately, the 28 is often thought of as similar to the .410; in fact they are vastly different, and the 28 delivers far better, far more consistent performance. The standard 28-gauge bore, nominally .550-inch in diameter, and the standard ¾-ounce shot charge suit one another beautifully. The shot column doesn't string much, especially with hard pellets, and it contains enough of them (about 440 No. 9s and about 260 No. 7½'s) to deliver efficient pattern densities out to about thirty-five yards. Patterns can get patchy much beyond that, because a 28 just doesn't hold enough shot for long-range work.

Years ago, Federal made one-ounce and, more recently, ⅞-ounce loads in 28-gauge, but neither made much sense. Increasing a shot charge without also increasing bore diameter is no improvement. Twenty-gauge loads belong in 20-gauge guns.

Those who like to gush about its virtues sometimes seem loath to admit that the 28-gauge has survived for reasons other than intrinsic merit. Merit it has, but the fact remains that if there were no 28-gauge event in skeet, there would be no 28-gauge. Witness the demise of 16. Intrinsic merit alone is not enough. A 28 is a wonderful target gun and, within its limitations, an equally good game gun, but the 20-gauge is more versatile, and current economic realities are such that no American maker can produce a true 28-gauge—by which I mean a perfectly proportioned double—at reasonable cost. As a separately manufactured item, the 28 simply cannot sell enough copies to support itself. Consequently, most of the readily accessible 28s are 20-bore guns with 28-bore barrels.

Which is not as lamentable as it might seem. A large measure of the 28's appeal is that it can be lightweight and still comfortable to shoot. The rule of thumb is that a gun should be at least ninety-six times heavier than the shot charge it fires. For the 28, that means a gun of at least 4½ pounds, which is enough to dampen recoil but not necessarily enough to point and swing consistently well. I've tried guns that light, but I'd hate to have to feed myself on the game I could bag with one. A 5½-pound gun, though, is another story, light enough to carry all day and still heavy enough to handle with control. That's where the 28-gauge truly shines.

10

Striking a Balance

Of all the things that influence the way a shotgun handles, none are more important than stock fit and balance. You don't have to look far to find all the treatises on stock fit you care to read, but balance is often glossed over, offered as a prescription, ignored altogether, or made to seem as arcane as alchemy, as exotic as voodoo.

There's no great mystery about balance, although there is a certain magic in its results.

Balance is simply weight distribution, how a gun's overall heft is arranged in relation to the shooter's hands. Its effects can be profound, because the placement of weight can make a heavy gun seem light and a light gun seem clumsy, and some surprisingly small variations can make an enormous difference in how well you shoot.

The longer I fool with guns the more convinced I am that most shooters are more adaptable to stocks than to balance. Most of us grew up shooting guns stocked to factory specifications, and we've learned to make minor, unconscious adjustments to stocks that aren't an ideal fit. Give any reasonably good shot an unfamiliar gun and he'll soon adapt to the stock, assuming it's not greatly different from the one he's accustomed to.

Give the same man a gun with a different balance and he may never learn to shoot it well, even a gun stocked to his fit down to a gnat's whisker. I've seen it happen. It's happened to me.

The reason for this, I believe, is that our response to balance is wholly subjective. A good fitter can tell you what stock dimensions are correct; no one can prescribe the perfect balance. You're the only one who knows how a gun's dynamics feel to you, and the same gun is apt to feel different to me.

According to the classic concept, the gun's weight should be evenly distributed between the shooter's hands. Even though a number of writers (most of them British) have offered very specific opinions as to where the balance point should be, none of their prescriptions hold much water—simply because every shooter holds his gun a bit differently. Some crowd the trigger guard, others don't. More important, some take a long hold with the forward hand, some a short one, and others grasp the barrels somewhere in between. "Between the hands" is a variable, not a point that necessarily can be predetermined.

Experience leads me to view "between the hands" as more a point of departure than an ultimate goal in refining balance. If you start with an even distribution and tip the balance one way or the other, the effect can be dramatic. Shift the weight toward your trigger hand and the gun becomes a quick starter. At the same time, unfortunately, it also becomes a quick stopper.

In the art of wingshooting, the forward hand—the one that's holding the barrels—is the key. Where that hand goes, so goes the shot. Therefore it seems to me that the most effective balance places the weight between the hands and then adds just a smidgen in the front, overbalances the gun a wee bit toward the muzzle. How much depends upon how far you extend your forward hand, but I'm convinced that having a slight majority of the weight in the leading hand promotes the smoothest, most dynamic swing and follow-through.

Here's why. By far the most common places to miss a moving target, be it feathered or clay, are below and behind. Different stock dimensions can help overcome the tendency to shoot low, but only the leading hand can solve the problem of shooting behind. Anything that helps carry that hand through the target and helps keep it moving is an advantage. So is anything that helps you swing smoothly; you may have the forward allowance exactly right, but if the barrels are bobbing and jerking, you can count on a miss.

Some extra weight out front accomplishes both. The heft helps smooth out your swing, and the inertia tends to keep your forward hand moving—all of which will make your shooting more effective.

One of the simplest ways of shifting a gun's balance in a useful fashion is to choose one with long barrels. To my mind, the worst-balanced guns in the world are the current crop of short-barreled, light-nosed game guns, especially the small bores. If I had my way, 28 inches would be the minimum length for every set of 20-gauge barrels. If I were having a 28-bore built to order it'd have 29- or 30-inch barrels. It's radical thinking, and you're probably skeptical, but I'd bet a hundred dollars against a handful of spent primers that if I had such a gun and you tried it, you'd want to buy it.

We can all grow old and gray waiting for the firearms industry to dig itself out of the short-barrel mindset it's been in since World War II ended, but if you currently own one of these short-nosed pieces and aren't entirely happy with the way you're shooting, you do have some options.

A word of good advice: If you're six-foot-three, built like a pro linebacker, and are still waiting to start the honeymoon with your five-pound bird gun, don't waste your time. The best thing you can do is sell it and buy a gun that's more your size. You'll be happier in the end.

Assuming you're of more average size and build, and assuming you have a gun whose stock fits reasonably well, there are some good ways of experimenting with the balance. You can shift the balance of a repeater by replacing the wooden or plastic magazine plug with a length of brass or steel, although most repeaters are naturally balanced toward the muzzle anyway—which is one reason why the most deadly wingshot you ever knew probably used a Model 12.

The trick in changing a double gun's balance is to lighten the butt rather than add weight at the other end, and it's done by hollowing out the stock.

As the first step, tape some lead weights to the underside of the barrels just ahead of the fore-end. A couple of ounces will do to start. Then spend an afternoon shooting targets using your field-shooting technique, and experiment as you go, by adding and subtracting weights. You'll soon find the magic point, where any more weight out front feels sluggish and any less feels whippy. You'll know when it's right.

Then find the exact balance point by hanging the gun in a loop of thin (but strong) cord, and mark that spot on the gun with a grease pencil or something similar. That done, take off the barrel weights, remove the heelplate or pad, and bore some wood out of the stock with an auger bit or enlarge the drawbolt hole with a sharp chisel. Recheck the balance periodically, and when it balances at the point you've marked, you're finished. (But remember to check it with the heelplate or pad back on.)

If you're hesitant about doing this yourself, take it to a stocker once you've found the right balance point. It's not a big job and shouldn't be expensive—although it'll cost more if your gun has a plain, checkered butt, because the stocker will have to plug the hole and recut the checkering.

Don't fret about weakening the stock. Chances are you won't have to remove all that much wood anyway, and if the work is properly done a stock can be hollow clear to the wrist and still be perfectly strong. A few months ago, my friend David Trevallion showed me a Purdey stock on which he'd performed a radical hollowectomy; from the grip back, it was nothing but a shell with walls about an eighth-inch thick. He put the heel-plug in place, laid the stock on his workshop floor and stood on it. Both feet. Then I stood on it. I wouldn't have believed it if I hadn't seen it with my own eyes.

You might be equally surprised at how shifting a few ounces of weight from the butt to the barrels will suddenly make a jumpy, jittery gun feel controllable. And once you get control with your leading hand, I think you'll be pleased at how much more consistently you can put the shot where the bird is.

11

A Fitting End

Like everything else, the gun world owns its share of adages and aphorisms, wise and pithy saws that render certain truths to their essence. My favorite among them goes thus: The metal men make a gun fire, but the stocker makes it shoot.

I don't know who coined this little jewel, only that it came out of the English gun trade. No doubt it was the work of some stockmaker whose flair for words was at least as good as his skill with chisel and gouge. What I know for certain is that it's absolutely true. Those who build the locks and the barrels and all the other mechanical bits are the ones who make a gun go bang. But there's a difference between making noise and shooting, since the whole point of using a gun is to hit something now and then. So, the stocker makes it go bang where the shooter wants it to, and he does so by making the gun fit the gunner.

I daresay that everyone who's ever strung more than three words together on the subject of shotguns has tossed around references to gun fit. Which is all well and good; everybody knows a gun is supposed to "fit"—but what is fit, exactly? Why is it important? How can you tell if a gun fits, and if it doesn't, what can you do about it?

Essentially, fit is a matter of tailoring a stock so that your eye looks straight down the barrel or rib without your having to do anything but raise the gun to your cheek and shoulder. Simple enough as a concept, but as with so many aspects of shooting, the underlying principle is more complex.

It begins with the fact that we point a shotgun rather than aim it; that the act of wingshooting is an act of coordinated motion and not a seeking for pinpoint accuracy, as rifle shooting is. A gun should be an extension of the shooter; it should function as if it were an integral part of the leading hand and the pointing finger. Another name for this is eye-hand coordination—our ability to point a finger precisely at anything our eyes can see.

This natural gift requires only that the eye does not move—or, in shooter's terms, that you keep your head dead-still with your eyes focused on the target. To see what I mean, try this right now: Hold your head still, keep both eyes open, and point a finger at some small object across the room. Easy, isn't it? You can do it time after time and be right on the mark. But now move your head from side to side and try pointing at the same object. That's not so easy; imagine how hard it would be to get on target if your finger were a gunbarrel.

Keeping your head still is the first requirement for good shooting. You may have to move your feet in order to keep your balance during a shot, and you certainly will have to move your arms to bring the gun up and swing it. But if you move your head, you'll lose the key reference point between you and the target, and then everything goes out of whack.

Your cheek is the crucial point of contact between yourself and the gun—not your hands or your shoulder—because that's the point nearest your eye where the gun touches.

A gun that fits allows you to keep your head still when you shoot. All you should have to do is raise it to your cheek in order to be looking right down the rib. To accomplish this, the stock has to accommodate the length of your arms and neck, the shape of your shoulders and upper chest, the width of your face, the configuration of your cheekbone. If it does this, the gun will feel like an extension of yourself, and the act of getting your eye aligned with the rib will feel effortless and natural.

Although it serves a fairly complex purpose, stock fit is a function of relatively few dimensions—length, drop (bend, the English call it), cast, and pitch. The ideal way of learning what measurements are best for you is to have a session with a good gunfitter, perhaps using a try-gun, which is a gun with a fully adjustable stock. Unfortunately, gunfitting is not widely practiced in this country, and good fitters are hard to find. This isn't to say you should despair of ever finding a good fit, because you can learn a lot on your own.

One of the most persistent myths in gunning is that you can determine your proper stock length by tucking the gunbutt into the crook of your arm; if your index finger can reach the trigger with the gun held this way, the length supposedly is right. I haven't a clue how this got started, or when or why, but I can tell you it's utter nonsense. All it does is measure the length of the stock against the length of your forearm, and since you don't hold the gun that way to shoot, it doesn't mean a bloody thing.

I can also tell you that the typical factory stock is too short for at least 80 percent of the people who shoot. Factory standard is about 14¼ inches from the trigger to the center of the butt, and that will comfortably fit someone who stands about five-foot-six to five-foot-eight. If you're taller, you'll find yourself holding the gun so your trigger hand is comfortably distant from your nose and rolling your shoulder forward into the butt. This binds your arms and tempts you to move your head, both of which inhibit your ability to swing the gun smoothly along the target's track.

So what's the right length? It depends upon how long your arms are, for one thing, but mostly upon where you place your leading hand. You can make a short stock feel long by extending your leading hand farther toward the muzzle, and make a long one feel shorter by grasping the gun closer to the breech. Even if you shoot with your leading hand well out on the fore-end or barrels—which I hope you do, because that's how you'd point a finger and therefore the most accurate way of pointing a gunbarrel—a standard factory stock is probably still too short. As a point of reference, I stand just a skosh under six feet, wear a thirty-three-inch shirtsleeve, and shoot best with a stock that's 15¼ inches long—and I can shoot just about as well with one that's sixteen inches.

You can find your best length by holding the gun with your normal leading-hand position and, without moving anything but your arms, raise it until the comb touches your cheek. If the butt doesn't reach your shoulder, you need more length. You can determine how much by using a slip-on buttpad with some cardboard spacers inside; keep adding length until the butt touches your shoulder at the same time the comb touches your cheek. Don't be afraid of getting it too long. If you have to push the gun away from you just a bit, so much the better; that frees up your arms, and your arms should be doing all the work of moving the gun. Better your stock should be a bit long than too short.

The pitch of a stock is the angle of the butt relative to the line of the barrel, and its purpose is to bring the entire surface of the butt into even contact with your shoulder. What that angle should be depends upon the shape of your shoulder and upper chest. Too little pitch makes the toe of the stock dig into your pectoral muscle. This makes recoil more painful; it also prompts you to raise the barrel and shoot high. Too much pitch brings only the heel in contact with your shoulder, makes the gun slide around under recoil, and often sends the shot low.

You can experiment with pitch the same way you experiment with length—by adding small spacers into either the heel or the toe of a slip-on pad. What you're seeking is the angle that creates full and even contact with your shoulder when your eye is looking right down the rib.

Bend and cast are far and away the most important dimensions, because they directly affect the critical relationship between the gun and your eye. If they're right, you won't have to move your head even a fraction.

You can get a rough idea of how your gun fits, or doesn't fit, in the living room. Focus your eyes on some spot in the distance, keep your head still, and raise the gun to your cheek. If you aren't looking straight down the barrel and pointing at that spot when the stock touches your cheek, something needs to be changed. If all you see is the top lever or the back of the receiver, you need a higher comb; if you see the whole rib, you want a lower one. If the barrel's pointing to the left, you need some cast-off, which means the whole stock needs to be bent to the right. If you're pointing to the right, it needs bending left. (Think of a shotgun stock as the equivalent of a rifle's rear sight. The drop controls elevation, the cast controls windage, and you adjust where it shoots by moving it in the direction you want the shot to go.)

Years ago, English gunmaker and shooting instructor Robert Churchill devised a method that not only points up errors in fit but also offers specific prescriptions for correcting them. You'll need a patterning board of some sort; a steel plate freshly brushed with white paint is best, but you can get by with a wooden frame and a few sheets of butcher paper. You need to stand exactly sixteen yards back from the plate—this is important, so measure off a precise forty-eight feet; don't just pace it.

Mark a spot about an inch in diameter in the center of the plate, load your gun, and stand so that your eyes are directly above the sixteen-yard mark. Hold the gun in level ready position, focus your eyes on the spot, and in one smooth motion raise the gun and fire, without moving your head. Don't rush, but don't dawdle either. Above all, don't aim the gun. We are supremely adaptable creatures when it comes to gunstocks, able to fit ourselves to guns of all sizes and shapes, but the point of this exercise is to see where your gun shoots when you don't move your head or roll your shoulder or do any of the things we do to accommodate guns that don't fit.

Fire three or four shots this way and then have a look at the plate. If you've mounted the gun consistently, all the shots should have gone to the same place. If the patterns are centered on the spot where you were looking, your gun fits. If they aren't, measure the distance from the center of the pattern to the center of the spot, and that will tell you which direction your stock needs to be moved and how much.

The mathematics are simple enough: Each inch of variation at sixteen yards corresponds to one-sixteenth-inch at the stock. If your gun consistently centers patterns three inches low and two inches right, the comb needs to be $^{3}/_{16}$-inch higher and bent $^{2}/_{16}$- or $^{1}/_{8}$-inch left.

In cases of too much drop, you can make temporary adjustments much the same way you increased the length, by sticking a layer or two of moleskin onto the top of the comb. In other cases, you'll need to rely on a good stock man to make adjustments by shaving or bending. In any case, your goal is to come up with a gun that shoots right where you look.

The same approach works with any gun, with one exception. A side-by-side double is subject to a phenomenon called muzzle flip, a response to recoil that causes the barrels to flip downward as the shot charge travels down the bore and out the muzzle. As this flexure is enough to alter the path of the shot swarm, it's important that a side-by-side be tailored to shoot slightly higher than an over-under. In the classic arrangement, a side-by should print about two-thirds of its shot swarm above the point of hold at thirty or forty yards and about one-third of it below. By mitigating muzzle flip, this will deliver the same practical performance as an over-under stocked to center its shot charge on the point of hold. Pumps and autoloaders don't seem subject to flip, so they, too, can be stocked to shoot right to the point of hold.

Tailoring a gun to fit doesn't necessarily mean having a new stock made. Factory stocks can be altered in all sorts of ways—shortened; lengthened with a recoil pad or a wooden extension; bent up, down and sideways; shaved; spliced; you name it. Working on your own, without the services of an expert fitter, may require some trial and error and some revisions before the job is right. Having a properly fitted stock may require that you change your shooting technique a bit and unlearn some of the things you've had to do in adapting yourself to your gun. But it will make a difference in your shooting, and that will make it worth the trouble.

12

Steamwhistles and Screw-Ins

The French have a lovely aphorism: *Le plus ce change, le plus c'est la même-chose.* Translated, it means: "The more things change, the more they remain the same." That is as true in the shotgun world as it is in any other.

It's also true that the shotgun world is as fond of fads as teenage kids are fond of hair and of using it to show how different they are from the generation that came before them. It's about as hard these days to find a kid who doesn't sport a fool's tail as it is to find a shotgunner who doesn't believe that interchangeable choke tubes are the be-all and end-all of shooting.

The rebelliousness of youth is probably as old as hair itself. Variable choking in a shotgun is somewhat younger, but not much, since the notion came into being almost simultaneously with the discovery of choke boring. Like most fads, the latest has a decidedly old flavor to it.

The first variable choke system for a shotgun is described in a patent issued April 10, 1866, to Sylvester Roper of Amherst, Massachusetts. The patent covers a repeating breechloader that left no lasting impression on firearms evolution, but one feature of it proved to be a hundred years or more ahead of its time.

While others concentrated on squeezing down a section of the bore itself, Sylvester Roper concluded that there is no reason why choke has to be an integral part of the barrel. He threaded the outside of his gun's muzzle, machined some short tubes with various degrees of inside taper, and so allowed a hunter to alter the reach of his gun simply by removing one tube and screwing on another.

Unfortunately, Roper's repeating gun was a cumbersome thing that would function only with milled-steel cartridge cases of Roper's own design, and the whole thing, ingenious choke tubes and all, soon faded away.

A few British gunmakers also explored ways of adding choke after the fact. John Rigby and William Middleditch Scott—namesakes, respectively, of Rigby's and W&C Scott—collaborated in 1875 on a patent for tubes that fit over a muzzle. In 1880 J.S. Heath patented an "attachable muzzle"—actually a pair of tubes meant to be fitted to a double gun. Thomas Turner of Birmingham bought rights to this patent about 1883 and in his advertisements said of the device: "Guns fitted with this invention can be converted from cylinder to choke, or vice versa, in one minute, while in the field. The muzzle can be easily carried in the waistcoat pocket..."

Although a number of people in both England and America experimented with variable chokes of one sort or another, no system gained any widespread acceptance until the 1930s, when Colonel Cutts of the U.S. Marine Corps came up with what would be known as the Cutts Compensator—an astonishingly ugly but certainly effective gizmo that comprised a ventilated cage about half again larger than barrel diameter and a series of choke-constricted screw-on tubes. Lyman bought manufacturing rights and turned out Cutts Compensators by the carload. Just about every skeet shooter of the 1930s and '40s had one on his favorite target gun; hunters were fond of it, too. A modified version of the Cutts was even used as a muzzle-brake on the Thompson Submachine gun.

At about the same time, E. Field White tried a different approach and designed the famous Poly-Choke. Instead of interchangeable tubes, Field used a single thin steel tube split into flexible petals. A tapped, tapered collet fits over this, and the degree of choke is adjusted by screwing the collet tighter or backing it off, compressing the petals or allowing them to expand.

Both devices proved popular enough to spawn a spate of imitations from the 1940s through the early '60s. By and large they tended to fall into two groups, either designed like the Cutts with separate tubes or as collet-type affairs like the Poly. In 1940 the Weaver Scope Company brought out the Weaver Choke—a ported compensator with half a dozen screw-on tubes. Pachmayr sold a similar device called the POWer-PAC, and Simmons Gun Company, the vent-rib outfit, had its own version for a few years in the 1950s.

The Poly-type ultimately was the more popular, probably because it has no separate tubes to fool with and also because it is capable of almost infinite adjustment. Herter's, Mossberg, and Savage-Stevens all offered variations on White's design. The Shooting Master, manufactured during the 1950s, was another of the same type, as was the Cyclone, made by the Hartford Gun Choke Company.

Inevitably, some really hard-core tinkerers got into the act and came up with self-adjusting chokes. The Jarvis Choke probably was the earliest of these, followed by the Adjustomatic from the Hartford Choke Company and by a similar offering from Poly-Choke. All of them were collet types, and all automatically stopped down their muzzle constriction by one step after the first shot. If you set the device at improved-cylinder for the first shot, the second would be through a modified choke. And if the first setting was modified the next was a full-choke shot, and so on. I have no idea whether they really worked. Mercifully, none has been on the market for years.

The add-on devices, obviously, are best suited to single-barrel guns, but there always are some who refuse to be distracted by the obvious. I have in my files a clipping from the September 1935 issue of *National Sportsman,* showing a pair of Cutts Compensators mounted on the muzzles of a side-by-side double gun. It comes close to qualifying as The Damnedest Thing I Ever Saw.

It took a surprisingly long time for anyone to rediscover Sylvester Roper's idea, and even then it came with a false start. In 1961, ninety-five years after Roper's patent, Winchester developed the Versalite Choke for the ill-fated Model 59 shotgun, the autoloader with the fiberglass barrel. The gun itself was a flop, not because of any intrinsic flaw but simply because few gunners were inclined to accept a shotgun with anything other than a traditional solid-steel barrel. But the Versalite Choke was another matter, and it brought the evolution of interchangeable chokes a step closer to what is common today.

The Versalite is a sort of one-piece Cutts Compensator designed in reverse. It has an integral choke tube and ported cage, but the tube is at the rear instead of the front, and it fits inside the muzzle. The compensator portion is of barrel diameter, so when the device is in place it simply looks like a gun with a ported muzzle—a nifty idea but one still ahead of its time. The Versalite disappeared from production along with the Model 59 in 1965.

Four years later the idea came back, this time in essentially its final form. Winchester introduced the Winchoke system in 1969, available for both the Model 1200 pump gun and the Model 1400 autoloader. It is the old Versalite without the compensator—a choke tube that screws inside the barrel, leaving only a thin, knurled ring extending past the muzzle. It's still in production. Stan Baker of Seattle, who in 1975 became the first barrelsmith to offer custom-fitted choke tubes, uses a similar design.

The obvious final step was a tube that fit entirely inside the muzzle. No doubt some firearms historian of the future, with a taste for tracing the obscure, will learn exactly who made the first ones. Browning probably was the first factory to do so, and Jess Briley of Houston probably was the first custom gunsmith to make them. Today, any gunmaker with even the slightest interest in the latest trends offers some sort of choke-tube system, and there are at least a half-dozen custom shops around the country that can fit tubes to virtually any gun you care to bring in.

Theoretically, the ability to change a shotgun's chokes to accommodate every sort of game and habitat is a great notion. That's been the main selling point for every variable choke design since Cutts's, and the people who are dedicated to such things will be happy to tell you what whiz-bang items they are. But the bottom-line question is seldom asked and even less often answered: What good are they, really?

I have no more quarrel with the idea of variable chokes than I have with the idea of single selective triggers, but I can't work up much enthusiasm for the reality of either. Theory aside, my experience has been that a selective trigger, especially on a game gun, is as useless as a shot glass at a WCTU convention. You set it to fire the open-choke barrel first and let it go at that. Single triggers themselves are fine, but the selective feature is just one more gadget to go wrong.

Similarly, choke tubes seem to me more useful in theory than in practice. I've not yet met the man who carries a pocketful of tubes and a wrench into the field, changing chokes every time he walks from a grainfield into the woods and then back again. It might be fun to think about, but nobody does it.

Which isn't to say that there aren't some good reasons to have a gun fitted with tubes. It's just that the best reasons are seldom the ones you hear about.

For one thing, choke tubes are a great feature to have on a gun that fits. In my opinion, American shotgunners pay too much attention to choke and too little to stock fit, but if you put the two together, then you truly can enhance a gun's versatility. You won't shoot well with a gun that doesn't fit, no matter what the chokes are or how many ways you can change them. But if you can fine-tune the fit of one gun and become thoroughly accustomed to its dynamics, choke tubes will give you the added advantage of having optimum chokes for any game.

If you travel to hunt, as I sometimes do, you know what a pain it can be to drag along—and worry about—several guns. It's not uncommon for me to hunt woodcock and ducks on the same trip, which means taking a main gun for upland work, a backup in case something breaks, and yet a third for wildfowl. With one perfectly fitted gun and some tubes, you can pare down your gear a bit.

Another practical advantage is that choke tubes can breathe new life into an old favorite waterfowling piece. Today we all have to use steel shot for ducks and geese, so if your old pet is too dear to part with, Jess Briley can give it a set of stainless-steel tubes that will handle steel without the risk of bulging the muzzles or popping the ribs loose. Among the classic doubles, the best candidate for that treatment is the old Super-Fox; there never was a better wildfowl gun. Some of the Parkers and Smiths and Ithacas might do as well, but none will stand up to the pounding of steel-shot ammunition as well as a Super-Fox will.

The key factor in any add-on choke device, whether it's inside the barrel or fastened onto the end, is how well it's installed. If the choke tube is not precisely concentric with the bore, the shot swarm's point of impact will be someplace other than where it ought to be. A lot of shooters learned that the hard way after having some shade-tree gunsmith put on a Cutts or a Poly, and the same principle applies to internal tubes. If you have any gun fitted with tubes, it's extremely important to find a gunsmith who'll guarantee no change in the point of impact, and equally important to test the gun on a patterning board as soon as you get it back. It's a good idea to pattern-test even a new gun that has tubes; any factory can turn out an occasional clunker.

On the other hand, a really good chokesmith can deliberately alter a gun's point of impact by boring the chokes eccentrically. I believe Bob Brister and Jess Briley, working together, were the first to put that notion into practical use. But except for some highly refined special-purpose guns, it seems to me the better course to order the tubes installed concentrically and refine the point of impact with a well-fitted stock.

Choke tubes are a fine idea so long as you realize that no shotgun can be completely versatile without a trade-off. Choke is only a small part of what makes a gun truly well suited for any particular use. With tubes, you can give a lightweight upland piece enough reach for geese, but that doesn't make it a good goose gun—certainly not a comfortable one to shoot with heavy loads nor one with the best dynamics for long-range shooting. By the same token, being able to put a skeet tube into an eight-pound duck gun doesn't mean you have the ideal tool for woodcock or grouse. There's more to it than a few thousandths of an inch muzzle constriction more or less. No matter how we might change the parts, the whole is going to remain much the same.

13

Practical Chokes

Something I notice in spending time around people who shoot: hand an American an unfamiliar gun, and the chances are about seven thousand to one that within the first sixty seconds he'll ask how it's choked.

I notice, too, that a lot of us seem to choose new guns according to how they're choked (or what screw-in choke tubes are available) rather than how they're stocked or balanced.

We are, if not truly obsessed, at least profoundly preoccupied with choke. What else explains the gallons of ink spilled in endless discussion of the "best" chokes for every shooting situation? Or the fact that even the most cryptic classified-ad description of any gun inevitably makes a point of letting us know how it's choked? Or that factories and custom shops alike enjoy a thriving trade in fitting, retrofitting, and tailoring screw-in choke tubes for virtually everything that shoots?

Face it, we spend an inordinate amount of time and energy fussing over the interior dimensions of the terminal three or four inches of gunbarrels, dimensions measured in the thousandth-part of an inch. I say "we" because in my experience, shooters in other parts of the world pay relatively little attention to choke. (Trap and pigeon shooters are the exception, but serious trap and pigeon shots everywhere are known fussbudgets anyway and therefore make up a subset unto themselves.) The fact remains, as a shooting culture, we Americans are a choke-happy lot.

The question is why, and according to what principle? The first part is complicated. The second is not. To understand the American view, compare the British system of describing degrees of choke with ours: what the English call quarter, half, three-quarter, and full chokes, we call improved-cylinder, modified, improved-modified, and full. Clearly, we believe more is better, that cylinder and modified bores can be "improved" by making them tighter. Cast the same attitude the other way around and we'd call them "degraded full" and "impaired modified." It's the same line of thinking that believes more powder and more shot make a more efficient cartridge. But even those enlightened gunners who recognize the fallacies in the heavy-load proposition often remain hung up on choke.

Actually, we come by this preoccupation honestly, and it's one once shared by all the world. The notion of constricting the nose-end of a gun bore to improve its performance is almost as old as the gun itself. In its modern incarnation, choke-boring was rediscovered more or less simultaneously in the 1860s and '70s by William Rochester Pape, W.W. Greener, and Fred Kimble. It's been all the rage ever since.

Exactly how choke works is still not perfectly understood. Covering all the facts and theories of applicable physics, mechanics, and geometry would make an interesting, if somewhat ponderous book. Instead, let's take the fact that it *does* work as a given, and talk here about practical application and the importance of choke to a bird hunter and recreational target shooter. Why, in other words, are we so concerned about choke, and does the actual effect justify all the attention and fret?

There's no question that choke originally served a genuine purpose—which was to compensate for inefficient ammunition. Semi-explosive propellants are brutally hard on shot, and both black and early nitro powders gave shot columns a savage pounding at the moment of ignition, instantly knocking a certain number of pellets in the charge out of round. With no shot collars to protect them on the way down the bore, other pellets got scraped flat-sided against the barrel wall. Standard shot charges were relatively light, only 1⅛ ounces even in 10-gauge, so the loss of even a small number of pellets from the effective swarm took a serious toll on pattern density at all but point-blank range.

Ammunition-makers did not yet have the materials or the understanding to improve cartridges, so gunmakers used choke-boring to keep the undamaged pellets closer together at greater distance.

This is an essential point, and it warrants emphasis: The only pellets that contribute anything to efficient ballistics at any great distance are those that fly true and retain maximum energy. The fewer of these you have to work with, the more important it is to keep them closely bunched as long as possible. Choke, therefore, was meant to act primarily upon the pellets that managed to get out of the case and down the bore relatively unscathed. Choke alone never has been able to reduce the number of misshapen pellets or make them any more useful.

If ammunition were no better than it used to be, choke would be as important as ever. But shotshells have undergone a profound evolution. It began right after World War I, when John Olin developed a progressive-burning nitro powder that shoved rather than slammed shot charges down the barrel; it went forward with even gentler powders created along the same lines and with the development of shot highly alloyed with antimony. The watershed came in 1960—the year Kennedy stomped Nixon, a year before Yuri Gagarin became the first man to orbit the earth in space, and three years before anyone ever heard of the Beatles.

In that year of grace, Remington Arms introduced its SP-type cartridge and thereby sent choke-boring on the road toward obsolescence. The SP's slick, strong plastic case had something to do with it, but the nub of the revolution lay with what Remington called the Power Piston—a simple piece of molded polyethylene that performed three functions vital to an efficient cartridge: Its obturating skirt effectively sealed the bore to keep powder gases behind the shot charge, where they belong; its collapsible midsection helped cushion the pellets at the moment of ignition; and the tough petals of its shot cup kept a high percentage of the outer pellets from being scraped half-flat against the bore.

The one-piece shot-cup wad has since been incarnated in myriad forms. They're all variations on a common theme, and they represent the single most important factor in the evolution of shotshells since the self-contained cartridge. Combined with good powder and hard shot, it creates a level of efficiency that our grandfathers would never have dreamed possible. And as a side effect, it has made choke as outmoded as a celluloid shirt-collar.

This isn't to say that choke no longer works, but rather to suggest that we no longer have much need of it, and that in many instances it's more handicap than asset.

Sounds outrageous? Think about it. Right from the start of the shot-cup era, ammunition makers discovered that the new components increased pattern densities by about 10 percent—and 10 percent pattern density is what distinguishes one choke increment from the next. So a barrel regulated for improved-cylinder performance with old-style shells delivered modified patterns with the new ones. As time went on, newer powders and harder shot improved density even more dramatically. Gunmakers eventually began boring chokes with the new cartridges in mind, but the fact is, the best shells available nowadays are so efficient that they no longer need the kind of compensation choke was meant to provide.

Should we not then rejoice in having denser patterns and try to improve them even more by using plenty of choke? We should not. On the contrary, we should turn this enhanced density to real advantage and seek optimal pattern spread by using less choke than ever. This is especially true for upland bird hunters.

Remember, choke originally was meant to affect the center of a shot swarm, keeping that sector dense to make up for inefficiency at the edges. But now that we have more usable pellets in the swarm, that center can in effect be considerably larger and still be dense enough to reliably kill game and break targets.

To see the advantages of a larger pattern, consider that choke is in one sense a function of distance, and its purpose is to keep the shot swarm smaller in diameter at greater range. We still define degrees of choke according to the number of pellets that print inside a thirty-inch circle at forty yards. If your favorite quail gun will put half its shot in that circle at that distance, you'd say it had an improved-cylinder choke and call it a damn good quail gun. And it would be—at forty yards. At fifteen or twenty yards, it's throwing a pattern scarcely larger than a dinner plate, a pattern so dense that a well-centered bird is likely to disappear in a pink mist; so small that a tiny error in gun-pointing means a clean miss. For all practical purposes, you're shooting your quail with a full-choke gun.

But don't you need the choke for all those forty-yard birds? There are two answers to this. First, if you're an average upland hunter and an average shot, you don't shoot at many forty-yard birds, and you hit only a fraction of these. By far the majority of upland birds bagged in the United States die within twenty-five yards of the gun, most of them at twenty yards or less. The nature of our birds, their habitats, and the way we hunt all combine to make upland shooting a short-range affair. If you find this hard to believe, spend a season pacing distances and keep records; you'll be surprised at the averages.

Close-in work being the norm, our own experience conditions us to pass up most forty-yard birds as being out of range. Place a life-sized silhouette of a quail, pheasant, or dove at a measured 120 feet, and you'll see what I mean.

The second answer may be even harder to believe, but it's true: if you're using top-notch cartridges, you don't even need the choke at forty yards. With the best ammunition available today, a skeet- or cylinder-bore barrel will kill birds and break targets at distances most shooters find astonishing. This is a fact not widely appreciated—mainly because we shy away from longer shots in the first place, and when we don't, we blame the misses on choke instead of gun-handling.

Three or four of us were horsing around on a skeet field one afternoon, seeing how far we could back away from Station 4 and still break targets. Nobody hit them all, but one chap began missing at about thirty yards and by forty yards concluded that he didn't have enough choke—forgetting that the rest of us were shooting skeet guns, too. Standing behind him, I soon noticed that his gunbarrel tracked the targets nicely, got ahead, then suddenly lost momentum. The shots went consistently behind.

I asked how he thought the shot could be made, and he answered to the effect that his lack of choke demanded he center each target perfectly to have the hope of even getting a chip—thus confirming what I thought I was seeing.

Starting with the assumption that his gun really wasn't up to the task, he was doing what any of us would do—trying to be too precise, shifting his eyes from target to gunbarrel and back, attempting to measure lead right to the inch. When we do that, we aim the gun instead of simply pointing, inevitably check the swing and shoot behind.

It was an error in technique prompted by a lack of confidence in the gun. Once I talked him into keeping his eyes on the target and then looking well ahead of it, he started hitting and making good, solid breaks. And once he understood that the whole thing originated between his ears and not in the end of the barrel, he wasn't nearly so concerned about choke.

Jack Mitchell, to my mind the master shooting instructor of them all, uses a tower shot to demonstrate the fallacies in our assumptions about guns and chokes. Last spring, I joined a group of shooters he was taking through the exercise. A couple were shooting 20-bores, and one or two others had guns with little or no choke. The shot was a left-to-right crosser of medium height, and Jack walked us back until most agreed that the target was beyond the ability of both their guns and their shooting.

With a few minutes of good coaching, everyone was hitting, and the 20s were smashing targets just as well as the 12s. The disbelievers were flabbergasted—all the more so when we computed the actual distance of the shot. Knowing how high the trap was, we figured target height at twenty-two yards and measured the distance from its line of flight to where we stood at forty-five yards. A pocket calculator showed the distance from gun to target to be just a hair over fifty yards. Then Jack had us break a few more, just to make sure we got the point, and some people went away from it with a whole new outlook.

The gun industry makes its own assumptions about choke, the most unfortunate of which is that anyone who wants open bores also wants short barrels. This is unfortunate because it actually prompts some shooters to buy the wrong gun in order to get the right choke. Don't be tempted into such a bass-akwards approach. Stock fit, trigger-pull, gun dynamics, and good technique are infinitely more important than choke. If you have to accept tight bores in order to get a gun that really suits you, that's okay; any good gunsmith can open them up. If your gun has screw chokes, all you have to do is order an extra cylinder- or skeet-bore tube.

Traditional wisdom has it that a barrel with no choke shoots doughnut-shaped patterns, with big gaps in the centers. I don't know how this notion got started. Maybe it was true in the days of so-so ammunition, though I doubt it. I do know it isn't true any longer. Give me good cartridges with hard shot, and I can do just fine without choke. So can you.

14

Buying Smart

A few months ago, while strolling the exhibition hall at a hunters' convention with my friend McNally, a case on a gun dealer's table caught my eye. Any gun case is likely to pique my curiosity, but this was an oak and leather trunk showing the patina of many years, and confronted with one of those, I become much like the fabled gentleman of over-amorous inclinations of whom it's said that he would make advances to a birdcage if he thought there was a canary inside.

There was a canary in this one, a little bedraggled, but still a canary—a trim little 20-gauge with the name of a very famous gunmaker on the locks and an extremely prestigious London address on the rib. I asked the proprietor if I could take it out and, with his assent, looked it over for a few minutes, put it back, thanked him, and wandered on.

"I wish I had a notebook," McNally said.

"Why?"

"So I could write down all the things you did with that gun. Is it worth the price he's asking?"

"Nope. The rib's about to come loose, the action's off the face, and the stock-head may be split."

"Repairable?"

"Sure. Two or three grand should put it right as rain."

"That's what I mean," McNally said. "I could look at it for a week and not see anything wrong. You oughtta write something about how to spot problems in older guns, how to tell the difference between the jewels and the junk."

I'll leave it to you to decide whether I oughtta, but McNally was right on one count, at least: In the gun world, there's no jewel like an old one. Older guns touch me in ways that new ones usually don't. Like some women, they're all the lovelier for showing a bit of mileage, for looking as if they've been somewhere and done something, and gained some character because of it. There's no beauty quite like beauty shaped by time.

Unfortunately, time and use can exact a toll, and the effects aren't always readily apparent. (I'm talking only about guns here, and from here on. The mature-woman simile is apt to get me into trouble if I take it any further.) Some things are best evaluated by a good gunsmith, but that's the second step. The first is to decide whether the gun in question is worth a professional vetting or whether it's best left to become someone else's problem.

Among the proverbial lock, stock, and barrel, pay close attention to the barrels. They're apt to be the most expensive part to repair, certainly to replace. Deep dents and fat bulges are easy to see; small ones aren't, necessarily, but they show up better if you point the barrels toward a source of light, so their surface picks up reflection, and peer along their length as you rotate them. If you can get the straight-edged shadow line of a door- or window-frame reflected down their length as well, so much the better for seeing any waves, ripples, gentle bulges, or other such irregularities. Hold them at arm's length and sight down the rib to see if it's dented or crooked. If it shows jogs or bends, there's a good chance it has come loose and been resoldered at some time; putting one back on and getting it straight is a tricky job. If the rib has been reset, the barrels will have been reblued or blacked.

If the ribs don't show any evidence of having been reset, ringing the barrels will tell you if they might soon need to be. Hang the barrels on your finger by the lump, and strike them with a backhand flip of your fingernails. They should ring with a clear, sweet, bell-like tone. If they don't, if they sound dull and clunky, the solder holding the ribs on is beginning to crystallize, and something is likely to come loose in the near future. (On the other hand, you can make the best set of barrels in Creation sound like real dogs if you hold them by the extractors when you ring them. It's an old gyp-trader's trick to knock down the buying price. I mention this not to suggest that you do it, but rather so you won't have it done to you sometime.)

It's not always easy to tell if a set of barrels has been shortened. American barrels should measure precisely to the inch, not in fractions; those on European guns might not, because Europe operates on the metric system. The muzzles should be perfectly square in relation to the centerline of the rib, and they ought to be very close together, even touching—although the muzzles of ultralight small-bores might not.

Shortening barrels isn't always the kiss of death for the way a gun performs. Sometimes, all it does is eliminate the choke. But shortening also can change one barrel's point of impact. Shooting at a patterning plate is the only way to find out if that's happened.

English game guns have always been bored with 2½-inch chambers, and so were a lot of older European guns. The Continental pieces typically are marked with chamber length in millimeters—65 for 2½ inches, 70 for 2¾ inches. Some English guns have chamber-length stamps, but most don't. They are, however, marked to indicate the shot charge appropriate to their level of proof, so a stamp of "1⅛" on the barrel flats means 2½-inch chambers, and "1¼" means 2¾-inch.

The buyer's caveat here is that the stamps show how a gun was originally chambered, not necessarily how it's chambered now. A lot of them have been rebored to 2¾ inches, but unless the work was done in England, the gun won't be restamped nor, more important, will it have been reproofed. The problem is that removing steel from British barrels—through lengthening chambers, refinishing, removing pits, or whatever—can affect their integrity. It's wise to have a gunsmith measure the barrel walls of any older English gun you're thinking of buying, even one that appears pristine, and it's a necessity for a game gun that's been rechambered. Otherwise, you're taking a chance on buying an expensive pig in a poke.

If you find dents in the sides of the barrel lump up near the hinge-hook, someone probably has tried to tighten the action with a hammer and punch, a shade-tree approach that mercifully isn't as common as it used to be. Pass on any gun that shows such evidence.

In a break-action gun, the hinge is subject to wear, and no gun, no matter how meticulously built, is immune. Slamming the action closed, which all too many shooters do, only accelerates the problem and puts unnecessary stress on the fastening system besides. Wear in the joint ultimately affects the relationship between the barrels and the breech face; when gaps begin to show, which you can see by holding the gun up to the light, it is said to be "off-face." It may be off a little or a lot. A badly worn joint is easy to spot; the barrels will rattle around when the action is open, and often you can feel some play even when it's closed.

To detect lesser degrees of wear, take the fore-end off, hold the gun by the barrels, and thump the buttstock with the heel of your hand—on the sides, on top, all around. The more vibration you feel, the looser the joint. This test doesn't work very well if the gun is a self-opener (which includes all Purdeys) because the opening-assist springs keep the barrels tight against the frame even when the fore-end is off. For these, you need to hold the top lever all the way open, let the barrels tip just slightly, and flex them; you'll be able to feel any slack.

What to do about a gun with a worn hinge depends on how worn it is, what its condition is otherwise, how badly you want it, and how good a bargain it is. A gun that's slightly off-face will stand good service for a long time to come, and don't dismiss it out of hand even if it's badly off, because any gun can be rejointed.

Inspecting lockwork, ejectors, and such is a gunsmith's job, but a close look at the exterior will tell you how suspicious of internal problems you should be. Buggered-up screw slots are classic symptoms. They mean that some ham-fisted clod has been at work, and if he can't take out a screw and put it back without chewing it up, then anything he might have done inside probably wasn't done any better. Don't be surprised at what you find; one gunsmith recently told me of finding a lock that had been "repaired" with a safety pin.

Naturally you'll want to check out the functioning of any gun you're seriously considering, and you can get a good idea of what shape the locks and ejectors are in just by testing them with snap caps. You can check the sears by pulling the triggers with the safety on, then clicking it off without touching the triggers. If one locks or the other trips, you're probably dealing with a bad sear.

Try the ejectors one at a time and then together. Both should trip at the same time, just a fraction after the locks cock (you can hear the locks if you listen closely) and should toss the snap caps about the same distance. If one requires a hard jerk on the barrels, it's going to need some attention.

Wood being both more mutable and less durable than steel, stocks are heir to all kinds of ills—shrinking, swelling, splits, chips, rot from years of soaking with petroleum-based oil, you name it. I've never seen a gunstock infested with termites, but it wouldn't surprise me. Look for cracks behind the tangs, behind the plates if it's a sidelock, and in the wrist.

As with loose action joints, stocks offer a lot of options, and the same considerations apply. Many (probably most) problems can be remedied—including, if the stockmaker is really good, some that appear a total loss. Matters of fit usually can be accommodated by bending, lengthening, or shortening. And any gun can of course be restocked.

The little 20-bore that set McNally off on all this showed some of these problems. The barrels didn't ring well; it was just enough off-face that I'd be thinking about a rejoint job if the gun were mine; and there were hairline cracks behind the top tang and the right-hand lockplate. One crack is one crack; two visible cracks in that part of the stock may in fact be one big one.

This isn't to say that it was a gun to avoid. On the contrary, it would have been a good buy if the price were low enough to accommodate some repairs and still leave you with something reasonably worth what you had in it. And when you're buying an older gun to shoot, that really is the bottom line.

I told McNally all this, or most of it, while we browsed around the exhibition hall, and as we neared the last aisle, he said, "This is definitely something you oughtta write. Let's go find some place to sit down and you can tell me more, and we can have a couple of beers."

One thing about McNally—he's full of good ideas.

15

Buying Guns at a Distance

Whatever else the current boom in mail-order marketing has or hasn't done to improve the quality of life, it has infused the used-gun market with a great vitality. Buying guns via catalogues, phone calls, and the local post office hasn't the same charm as browsing through a well-stocked shop, but it has brought buyers and sellers together on a scale that no single gunshop could ever hope to match. Clearing-house publications like *Shotgun News* and *The Gun List,* catalogues put out by sporting-goods companies, and periodic mailings from private gun dealers have all combined to put sportsmen and collectors in touch with what amounts to a nationwide inventory of the best guns the world has to offer.

The process of buying a gun at long distance is a bit more complicated than making a purchase face to face, and there are certain requirements to be met. Some are a matter of law and therefore immutable; others simply are customs of the trade and can vary from dealer to dealer. In either case, it helps to know what to expect and what's expected of you.

Let's assume that you're a bird hunter with a hankering to own a fine old double gun. You have some choices in how to go about finding one. You can start phoning dealers who advertise in sporting magazines and ask what they have in stock that fits both your needs and your budget. Those who have printed lists describing their inventory will be happy to send them to you. Some dealers charge a small fee for these; others don't.

A better approach is to find a current copy of *Shotgun News* or *The Gun List* and study it carefully. Since literally dozens of dealers, large and small, advertise in one or both of these tabloids, this will give you an overview of a variety of guns in every price range.

Once you've found a promising candidate, call the dealer to see if he still has the gun and to get a more complete description. There are several things you can do at this point that will help matters go smoothly, especially if you've never worked with this dealer before.

If you want a more detailed description of the gun, it's important to ask specific questions that can be answered objectively. You have the right to expect that the description in his ad is accurate, but don't assume that it covers every detail. You should ask about whatever details are important to you—original finish, altered stocks, shortened barrels, chokes, chambers, whatever. You also should ask about any mechanical flaws. He should certify that the gun is in good working order, or he should point out any mechanical problems.

Don't pose subjective questions and expect that his answer would necessarily agree with yours. If he says the wood is beautiful and you think it's ugly, don't accuse him of misrepresenting the gun; beauty is a personal thing. Make your own subjective judgments when you have the gun in hand, and remember that you can return it without having to justify your decision to anyone.

Since you'll be sending the dealer a check for a gun you've never seen, the two of you need to agree on a period of time for you to examine the gun and decide to keep or return it. The inspection period customarily is three days, beginning the day you actually receive the gun. But don't assume that every dealer works that way. Ask how long an inspection period he allows and when it starts. If you know you'll need more time for some reason, say so and come to an agreement. It isn't fair to tie up the man's inventory or to assume that he won't mind if you keep it for two weeks because you had to leave town on a business trip. Establish an inspection period and stick to it.

If you're buying the gun to shoot, you'll naturally want to test-fire it, and if it's a used gun, the dealer probably assumes that you will fire it. Nonetheless, it's not a bad idea to mention that up front. He wouldn't want you to fire a mint-condition collector's piece, but there's little likelihood that you'll find such a gun through an ad anyway; the collector's market generally doesn't work that way.

There are several matters regarding money that you should establish at the outset. The most obvious is selling price. You already know from the ad what he's asking for the gun. If it's more than you can afford, pass it up; don't agree to one price in the beginning and expect to haggle once you have the gun in hand. It doesn't hurt to ask if the quoted price is negotiable, but if he says no, take his word for it.

The most important thing to remember is that there are no objectively established market values for used guns. Supply and demand control the prices. The various price guides in print are only guides, not gospel. Pay no more than you can afford, and don't lose your head over the idea of owning a famous name or because you're afraid you may never find another. Remember, too, that a professional gun dealer is in business to make a living, and he's entitled to a fair profit. There's no point in arguing. If you think he wants too much for some gun, don't buy it.

Once you agree on a price, you also should agree on refund terms. If you return a gun promptly and in exactly the condition it was in when you got it, you're entitled to an immediate refund. Some dealers make a tidy, unethical sum every year by holding deposits in a bank account and letting them draw interest for a month or two before making refunds. There isn't much you can do about it except to conduct no future business with any dealer who doesn't return your money straightaway. A week from the time you return the gun is plenty.

You also should discuss shipping costs. Most dealers add the shipping cost onto the selling price, but some don't, provided that you ultimately buy the gun. Agree up front how this is to be handled, and then you won't be surprised if you find the shipping fee either added to the bill or deducted from your refund. Naturally, if you return the gun, you're responsible for the cost of sending it back.

Once you've struck a deal, establish a reasonable time during which he'll hold the gun while your check makes its way through the mail. The two of you have mutual responsibilities here. It isn't fair to expect him to wait indefinitely, so don't agree to buy unless you can follow up right away. On the other hand, it will take a few days for your check and the necessary paperwork (or just the paperwork, if the dealer accepts credit cards) to reach him, and he shouldn't sell the gun out from under you if somebody walks in the next day and offers cash. It doesn't happen often, but it's happened to me; instead of a gun, I got my check back along with an utterly lame explanation. It was my first and last deal with that chap.

Under the requirements of the Gun Control Act of 1968, a licensed dealer may ship guns only to someone who holds a valid Federal Firearms License (FFL), and before he can send a gun, he must receive a signed copy of the recipient's FFL. If you don't have an FFL, you need to find someone who does and who is willing to take delivery of a gun in your name. If you belong to a gun club, ask an officer if the club has a license; many do, for the members' convenience. Perhaps a friend holds an FFL. If not, ask a local gun dealer if he'll receive the gun for you. Most are happy to oblige, since it represents no expense to them and no inconvenience other than phoning you when the gun arrives and filling out a form that transfers possession of it to you. A few sour-grapes types charge 10 percent of the purchase price; thank them politely and look elsewhere.

You can send the dealer a personal check along with the FFL, but you'll most likely have to wait until it clears before he'll send the gun. Expect him to cash the check as soon as it arrives; he's running a business, not a lending library for guns. You can speed things up considerably by sending a certified check or a money order in the first place.

If the dealer has up to this point treated you well, return the favor and give him a call when the gun arrives. Let him know you have it and that you'll call him back in two or three days with your decision. And do just that. Make a firm decision, within the inspection period you agreed upon, whether to keep the gun or return it, and either way, phone the dealer and let him know. It's a courtesy he'll appreciate.

Do not call him and try to renegotiate the price. If the gun isn't what you expected, return it. If he lowers the price of his own accord when you tell him you're shipping it back, then you'll have to decide for yourself whether to accept—but such tactics tell me that he knew he was overpricing it to begin with and make me wonder if even the reduced price isn't too much.

While you have the gun, examine it carefully, and if you're uncertain of something, ask an opinion of someone whose judgment you trust. Test-fire it if the dealer has given permission. Pattern it. Shoot some clay targets. Make sure everything works the way it should. But remember that you are fully responsible for the gun as long as it's in your possession. Drop it, lose it, gouge the stock, or dent the barrels, and it's your baby.

On the other hand, if the gun doesn't work properly, call the dealer and let him know. Don't assume he's trying to pull a fast one, and don't nitpick the gun to death. You knew you were buying a used gun, and used guns sometimes go wrong. If there's an honest problem, the dealer should be willing to have it repaired or should adjust the price accordingly. It does happen, and a reputable dealer will make it right.

If you choose to return it, clean it and pack it securely in the box it came in. Federal law allows a nonlicensed person to ship a firearm directly to a licensed dealer, gunsmith, or factory. Choose a reliable carrier, and insure the gun for the purchase price. I've had excellent results shipping guns via United Parcel Service.

I've also had excellent results, by and large, with the dealers I've chosen. The world has its share of slickers out for a fast buck, and some of them sell guns. But the real pros—the ones in it to make a living and not a killing—are a pleasure. If you haven't done business in the long-distance trade, ask around to see who has a reputation for square dealing. Remember that advertising is not the same thing as reputation. Anybody can buy a lot of splashy ads; the real professional has a lot of customers who keep coming back.

LEGEND

16

The Pinfire

In his journal for the year 1662, English diarist Samuel Pepys wrote of seeing "a gun to discharge seven times, the best of all devices I ever saw." And in 1664 he wrote: "There were several people by, trying a new fashion gun to shoot often, one after another, without trouble or danger, very pretty."

Very pretty, indeed. Only it's a pity that Pepys didn't take the trouble to describe the guns themselves, because they were among the forebears of the modern breechloader. Still, we can be virtually certain that what Pepys saw were flintlocks of some sort and that they came from France.

Although the modern game gun is literally a British signature, its central principles were not British inventions. Samuel Johannes Pauly, a Swiss artillery officer in Napoleon's army, was first to recognize self-contained ammunition as the key to building a truly successful breechloader. Pauly set up as a gunmaker in Paris in 1808 and presently invented a breechloading action for a pouch-type cartridge with a percussion primer inside. (Pauly's assistant, Johann Nikolaus von Dryse, later evolved this action into the Prussian needle gun, the precursor of the modern bolt-action rifle.)

In 1812 Pauly patented an action based on a hinged breechblock with internal hammers, designed for centerfire cartridges. He obtained an English patent on the idea in 1816, and fixed-barrel breechloaders were for some time a mainstream concept in French gunmaking, culminating in 1894 with the Darne. By then the mainstream of world gunmaking was set on an altogether different course—and that one, too, originated in France.

Casimir Lefaucheux, of 37 Rue Vivienne, Paris, was a third-generation successor to Samuel Pauly. Like his contemporaries, Lefaucheux built hinged-breech guns in the Pauly mold. In the early 1830s, however, he tried another approach, devising an action in which the barrels swung down on a hinge to expose the breeches. The idea was novel enough to earn a whole series of patents, the first issued in 1834.

A central problem in designing a break-action gun is finding a means of fastening barrels and frame together that is both easy to operate and durable enough to withstand years of use. Lefaucheux's solution was a lump of steel soldered under the barrels. The semicircular notch at one end fits a cross-pin in the action bar to form the hinge; the long notch in the other end is the fastening bite, engaged by a bolt inside the frame. The action lever lies under the frame and fore-end and needs only a partial turn clockwise to free the barrels.

Lefaucheux fitted his earliest break-actions with external nipples and used standard percussion caps to ignite the cartridges, which probably were paper or linen pouches of powder and shot. In 1836, however, he took out patents on a design for wholly self-contained ammunition and thereby changed the course of modern gunmaking.

The Lefaucheux cartridge comprised a brass-headed

paper case with a pin protruding from the side, just ahead of the rim. Inside the case, the pin's tip rested on a priming cap that contained fulminate—in effect placing the firing pin inside the shell instead of inside the gun. Pinfires, as they were called, weren't the first cartridges to have shot, powder, and a primer all in the same package, but they certainly were handier and more efficient than any that had gone before. They could be carried in pouch or pocket and quickly put into a gun; the shooter had only to make certain that the pins were pointing upward and fit into tiny notches in the barrels. With special tools for recapping and crimping, the cases were relatively easy to reload.

Lefaucheux's pinfires suffered somewhat from inefficient wadding, but another Frenchman, Houllier, patented a much-improved, gas-tight cartridge in 1846. (Essentially, Houllier invented the base wad.) After that, Lefaucheux's guns, combined with Houllier's shells, enjoyed great popularity in France and elsewhere on the Continent.

The guns—and probably quite a few of them—made their way to England, too, but the British gun trade was in no great hurry to be impressed by anything that came out of France. About 1850 the famous British sportsman Peter Hawker wrote: "Let me caution the whole world against using firearms that are opened and loaded at the breech—a horrid ancient invention, revived by foreign makers, that is dangerous in the extreme." William Greener, W.W. Greener's father, also thought the whole idea was utter rubbish, describing breechloaders as a "specious pretence" that "cannot be made sufficiently durable to yield any reasonable return for the extra expense and trouble attending their fabrication." Writing under the pseudonym "Stonehenge," J.H. Walsh in 1859 referred to the pinfire breechloader as the "French crutch gun."

At the time, the English commonly referred to syphilis as "French gout," so these may not be wholly objective opinions. The archly conservative Hawker hadn't even fully accepted the caplock as superior to the flintlock until about 1844. Greener carried his distaste for breechloaders to his grave in

1869. In any case, how fondly the older makers clung to the old ways hardly mattered, for by 1860 British sportsmen had grown infatuated with Lefaucheux's pinfire.

The groundswell began in 1851 at the Great Exhibition in London, where Lefaucheux's display attracted vast attention from the public. Joseph Lang, a gunmaker of Cockspur Street, London, liked the idea so well that he had his own version ready for customers by the time the next shooting season came around. Within a year there was no going back. The British trade, roused from its lethargy, took up the breechloading gun with a passion, and would, in scarcely more than a generation, create the world standards by which the game gun still is judged.

Although it ultimately proved to be a dead-end path in the evolution of the gun, the pinfire was the first to benefit from the trade's attention. Woodward, Purdey, Holland, Dougall, Dickson, Lancaster, Boss, Richards, Lang, Francotte, and other makers in Britain, France, Belgium, and Germany turned them out by the score.

Early on, pinfire cartridges were substantially cheaper than those of centerfire design, which no doubt helped offset some of their shortcomings. The exposed pin apparently was no particular safety hazard, although the pins sometimes bent, which usually caused a misfire. The most pernicious gremlin, as Geoffrey Boothroyd reports, was gas leakage around the notches in the barrels where the pins protruded. These notches had to be large enough to allow the pins to move when struck, so a tight gas seal was all but impossible in the first place; any wear only compounded the problem.

English makers soon improved upon Lefaucheux's original, single-bite fastening system. In 1859 Henry Jones of Birmingham patented a much more efficient variation using the Lefaucheux underlever. Jones filed a T-shaped notch into the barrel lump and mounted a similarly shaped bolt in the action bar. Swinging the lever a short distance clockwise simply turns the bolt out of the notches and allows the barrels to pivot down.

Since the bearing surfaces are filed at a slight angle, camming leverage provides a tight, durable lockup.

Gunmakers in France, Belgium, Germany, and Britain copied the Jones system to such an extent that it probably is the most common fastener among all the pinfire guns ever built. It was generally known in Britain as the English or "T" action; in France and Belgium it was called *fermeture à T*. The Germans called it the *Englischer T Doppelgriff*, particularly in later years, after someone improved the system even further by turning the forward-pointing Lefaucheux lever back the other way and wrapping it under the trigger guard.

The 1850s and '60s saw an extraordinary burst of creativity throughout the British trade. New actions, fastening systems, and lock designs appeared by the dozen, and a great many of them were first built as pinfires: the Jones action; James Dougall's famous Lockfast action, patented in 1860; Westley Richards' doll's-head fastener, patented in 1862; sliding-barrel systems of various kinds—the list goes on.

All of the early fastening systems required the shooter to lock the action manually. In 1858, however, a Frenchman with the unlikely name Francois Schneider, of 13 Rue Gaillon, Paris, patented the world's first snap-action—an underlever connected to a spring-loaded bolt that fitted into a notch in the barrel lump. All the shooter had to do was swing the barrels up, and the gun locked itself. Now, of course, virtually every break-open gun in the world is a snap-action; but in 1858 it was the cutting edge of gun design. Westley Richards built the first English version the same year, and before long, the principle was applied to nearly every sort of action that existed, including Henry Jones's T-grip. Most of these early snap-action guns were pinfires.

The pinfire's popularity in England began to wane in the early 1870s, supplanted by the centerfire system, which was both more convenient and more efficient. A great many pinfire guns were converted to centerfire, but a great many more, some of them superbly built, remained in service for a surprisingly long time. In 1896 John Dickson of Edinburgh built what surely was among the last pinfires made in Britain, but Eley continued to manufacture pinfire cartridges in both 12- and 16-gauge until at least 1935.

The pinfire endured even longer on the Continent, widely built in France and Belgium until about 1920. In Italy, Beretta offered pinfire guns in several grades as late as 1938.

Although quite a few guns made their way to this side of the water, the pinfire never was very popular in the United States, and since the American shotgun trade didn't really begin to thrive until well into the centerfire age, no pinfires were built here.

Nowadays the guns show up less often, and new cartridges aren't available anywhere. Cobbling up some pinfire cartridges out of modern plastic cases probably wouldn't be a difficult job, however. And I imagine that some of the old guns would be great fun to shoot, albeit a strictly black-powder proposition, since none of the English pinfires were proved for nitro powder, and most of the surviving guns are likely to be in fairly frail condition. Still, a good, representative pinfire gun would make a fine collector's piece for anyone interested in the origins of the modern game gun, especially since the pinfire is where it all began.

17

The Monstrous Horrendum

In the thirty-eighth year of Queen Victoria's reign London's main sewage system was completed, the first roller-skating rink in the city opened, the London Medical School for Women was founded, and the British Patent Office granted William Anson and John Deeley letters patent on a hammerless gun. It was, all things considered, a typical year, especially at the three-quarter point of the nineteenth century. Perhaps the most striking thing about it is that the world has become a vastly different place in the 120-odd years since.

But not entirely different. Wastewater handling and medical education have changed a great deal since 1875, roller skating less so, and the gun described in Patent No. 1756 almost not at all. Instead, it has become the most widely used action for break-open guns in all the world.

We know it generically as the boxlock. In 1875, and for quite a few years after, it was more commonly called the Anson and Deeley action, or simply A&D, mainly to differentiate the original from the spate of variations that subsequently appeared in England and elsewhere. But with few exceptions, the variations were exactly that, and virtually every boxlock action in the world owes its lineage to the single patent issued May 11, 1875. It was, by any definition, a seminal event.

To appreciate just how revolutionary the Anson and Deeley idea really was, consider where the sporting gun's evolution stood at the time. The breechloading concept had been rediscovered only about sixty years before, in France, and the English trade hadn't built any break-action guns at all before about 1852. The hammerless breechloader was newer still; it, too, appears to have originated in France, with a design patented by Adolphe Jean Victor Marcet in 1863. Some evidence suggests that George Daw of 57 Threadneedle Street, London, built a similar gun as early as 1862, but the first English hammerless breechloader to achieve real success didn't come along until 1871, built and patented by Theophilus Murcott of 68 Haymarket.

Moving the hammer from the outside of a lockplate to the inside was relatively easy. Finding a way to cock it was something else. A lever was the most obvious answer, and a number of variations on the lever-cocking principle appeared in the 1870s and '80s. Some used one lever to open the action and another to cock the locks; the most successful, following Murcott's lead, accomplished both with a single mechanism.

Although the lever-cocking approach works well enough, few gunmakers saw it as the ideal solution. After all, a break-action gun is itself one big lever, in which the barrels offer far greater mechanical advantage than any smaller lever could hope to have. The trick is simply to devise an efficient linkage between them and the locks.

Joseph Needham of Piccadilly claimed the first patent on a barrel-cocking system in April 1874 with a design adapted to both trigger-plate lockwork or conventional sidelocks.

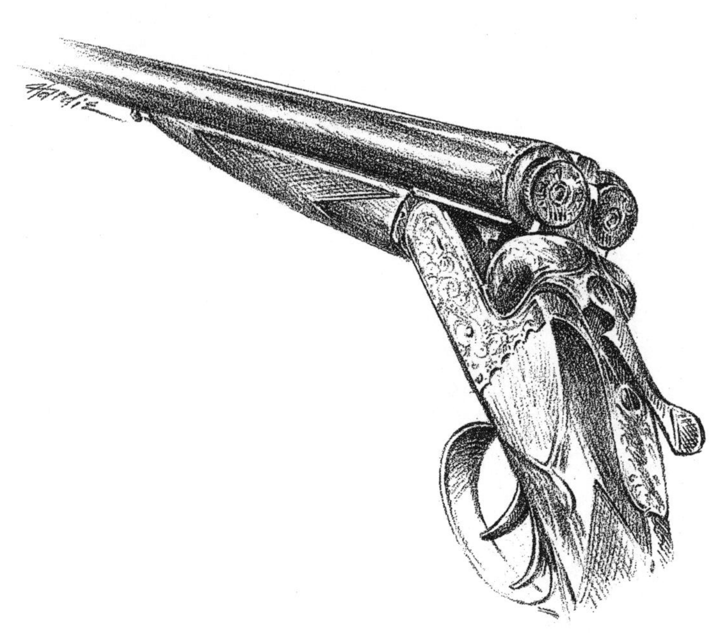

Needham's gun even had ejectors, all but unheard-of at the time, which makes it more significant still. Realizing that Needham was onto something, some other makers—notably Lancaster, Greener, and Churchill—happily paid royalties to build guns of their own on the same design. Nonetheless, history has been stingier with praise than Needham and his gun deserve, in no small part because of what Anson and Deeley did with the same concept a year later.

Needham's cocking piece is a short lever that extends into the water table slot just beyond the breech face. The rear edge of the barrel lump simply curves back underneath the lever and lifts it as the barrels drop down on their hinge. It's a simple approach, offers excellent leverage, and a number of gunmakers followed Needham's lead over the next twenty years. But the system is not readily compatible with an underbolt fastener—especially the Purdey-type double bolt, which even in the early 1870s was set fair to become a world standard—and even though its lineage didn't die out for a long time (both Parker and Lefever used variations of it), the Needham system never was a major influence.

In the Anson and Deeley system the cocking levers pivot on the same axis as the barrels. One end projects from the action knuckle and the other reaches back through the action bar to the tumbler. Leverage transfers via the fore-end iron, which leaves the barrel lump free to serve as part of the fastening system.

The concept obviously can be adapted to any sort of locks, but the Anson and Deeley gun packed a double whammy in that the lockwork was as revolutionary as the cocking system. It's brilliantly simple: a cocking lever, tumbler, sear, and mainspring make up the sum of each lock. Moreover, all the parts are attached directly to the frame rather than mounted on removable plates as in the then-universal sidelock system.

The mechanics of it almost certainly originated with Anson, who at the time was foreman of the actioning shop at Westley Richards in Birmingham. Deeley, who had joined the company in 1860 and had succeeded Westley Richards as managing director in 1872, provided the money and legal connections necessary to obtain the patent. The Westley Richards company, in turn, enjoyed the privilege of being the first and, for a time, sole manufacturer of the Anson and Deeley gun. Everyone involved profited even further by eventually allowing other gunmakers to use the design under license and royalty. This arrangement continued until the patent protection expired.

To say that the Anson and Deeley action caught the gunmaking world's fancy is an understatement, and tracing its subsequent history in any detail would amount to a fairly hefty book. Suffice it to say that by the turn of the century every gun trade on earth was building boxlock guns. Some were outright copies of the Anson and Deeley, others variations, more or less. Some makers, particularly Greener and Scott, devised patentable variations even while the original patent remained in force. As a result of their efforts—and of course those of Westley Richards—the whole Birmingham trade eventually came to be associated with the boxlock gun, leaving the more prestigious London trade the sometimes enviable job of perfecting the sidelock.

The American trade embraced the idea with a passion, and, apart from L.C. Smith, all of the great American names made their reputations with boxlock guns. Even Uncle Dan Lefever's masterpiece, the Automatic Hammerless of 1885, is not a true sidelock, although it is fitted with sideplates. In early Syracuse Lefevers (up to about serial number 25000), some lock parts are fastened to the sideplates, but after that, all the lockwork is mounted to the frames.

With the Lefever and some others, the American trade illustrates how amenable to variation the boxlock is and to what lengths gunmakers have gone in devising them—from the early Parker's Rube Goldberg mechanism to Ansley Fox's brilliantly simple three-piece locks and cocking system. Between lies a world of different approaches—cocking systems using levers, cranks, pushrods, cams, hooks, and sliding bars; fastening systems comprising underbolts, midbolts, top hooks, screws, crosspins, and shrouds; lockwork of every variety driven by springs of every possible form. You name it, and somebody has applied it to the boxlock gun.

From a gunmaker's perspective, simplicity is the boxlock's most endearing virtue, which may seem contradictory, considering some of the complex forms it's taken (the hammerless Parker from 1889 to 1917, for instance, or the Browning Superposed). But boxlocks don't have to be complicated. In the simpler versions, especially, the parts are easy to manufacture by machine, so the guns can be mass-produced at high levels of quality. Virtually every boxlock can be stocked in considerably less time and with much less hand labor than a sidelock. Actions and lockwork are similarly less labor-intensive to assemble. The list goes on.

Although boxlocks have been built from the beginning to best-quality standards, certain elements of the gunmaking and shooting community have tended to scoff at them as being somehow inherently second-rate. This attitude, originating from the old rivalry between the London and Birmingham gun trades, is, to a surprising extent, still around.

Although English gunmaking began in London, rich deposits of coal and iron ore in the Midlands made Birmingham an important manufacturing center as early as the Middle Ages, and the first records of guns built there date from the 1640s. In the 1850s, taking a leaf from American industry, the Birmingham gun trade was the first in Britain to adopt techniques of mass production and interchangeable parts, thereafter turning out military and sporting arms by the zillion.

While Birmingham clearly had the manufacturing advantage, the London trade held the trump cards: access to the vast majority of British wealth and complete control over the guns sold in and around the capital city of the Empire. A charter granted by King Charles I in 1637 authorized the Worshipful Company of Gunmakers of the City of London to establish rules of proof for all firearms. And further laws enacted in 1670 proscribed the sale of any unproved weapon within the environs of London. This in effect made the Gunmakers Company suzerain of the entire British trade: Anyone in the country could make guns, but only guns approved by the Company could be sold anywhere near London. It was a neat, highly effective stranglehold that certainly did not promote cordial relations between the London and Birmingham trades. And it lasted until the demand for military weapons reached such proportions in the late eighteenth and early nineteenth centuries that the London Proof House couldn't possibly keep up and Parliament established the Birmingham Proof House in 1813.

This, of course, did nothing to ameliorate the rivalry, even though the London trade was by then getting virtually all its components—barrels, actions, locks, and the rest—from Birmingham. The London makers, turning out fabulously beautiful, flawlessly hand-built sidelock guns for the nobility, thought the Birmingham makers little better than blacksmiths; the Birmingham makers, in turn, saw the Londoners as a parcel of overpaid and overrated snobs. In 1896 the famous game shot and amateur inventor Sir Ralph Payne-Gallwey summed up the prevailing London view this way: "...as a rule, that 'monstrous horrendum' a ready-made, reach-me-down Birmingham gun, is fit for neither man, nor bird, nor beast, and is a mere unwieldy log of iron and wood when compared to the perfect article produced in London."

Consider the fact that Sir Ralph's monstrous horrendum was almost sure to be a boxlock, and you can see where the snooty attitude toward them comes from.

Some, mainly Americans, have taken up the boxlock's banner and argued that it's actually the superior form, usually on grounds of durability. Sidelocks, they say, are inherently weak in the stock, allow grit and moisture readier access to their lockwork, break down more frequently because their parts are more delicate, and in general just aren't up to a steady diet of heavily loaded cartridges.

Sidelock fanciers counter by indicting boxlocks for being too heavy, having poor triggers, and lacking grace.

Except to those contentious sorts who can start an argument with a stump, there really isn't much point in debating generalities. Anyone who's seen more than a few guns knows very well that a first-rate boxlock is preferable to a third-rate sidelock and vice versa; so unless you're comparing guns of equal quality, all the clever reasoning and expert opinion in the world is just wind. But as I said, prejudices both ways still exist to a surprising degree. And some are worth considering—if for no other reason than to try to see where they come from.

That sidelocks have intrinsically weak stocks probably is the most widespread criticism, especially in this country, and if you judge solely according to the most famous American sidelock, there's something to it. L.C. Smith stocks have a definite tendency to split behind the top tang and at the rear of the sideplates, for several reasons. One is that there's too little bearing surface between steel and wood at the stock head and too much at the lockplates, which have square instead of chamfered edges. As the wood absorbs moisture from the air it swells against the plates and turns them into recoil lugs.

Smiths also tend to crack because most of them are stocked with American walnut, which is both more brittle and less flexible than European walnut. Smith used European wood only on its higher-grade guns. If you think about it you can probably remember seeing more cracked stocks on low-grade guns.

But not all sidelocks are L.C. Smiths, by any means. Those patterned after the London style—regardless of whether they're built in England or Belgium, France, Italy, Spain, or somewhere else, and assuming they're properly made—are as durably stocked as any guns can reasonably be. If they weren't, English sidelock double rifles wouldn't exist, certainly not as big-bores. Any stock design that can stand up to the recoil of .577 or .600 or even .700 Nitro-Express cartridges can handle shotgun shells till the cows come home.

In the same vein, moisture and dirt have no easier time getting into sidelocks than into boxlocks. If that were a real problem for sidelocks it would've shown up a long time ago in a climate as damp and rainy as England's.

The internal, working parts of boxlock guns do tend to be more robust than those in sidelocks, mainly because they can be. Lockparts mounted on a sideplate need to be slightly thinner so that a bit more wood can be left in the stock for maximum strength, but if the parts are properly hardened—or left relatively soft, depending upon their function—they're no more fragile than a ball-peen hammer. Cheap sidelocks and those made of poorly tempered metals (the two are not necessarily the same) do break down more often than they should. So do boxlocks made to the same quality or of the same sort of material.

Indicting sidelock guns, especially best-quality English guns, because they won't shrug off a boxcarful of hot-rock magnum cartridges is the unfairest cut of all—like condemning a Thoroughbred racehorse because it can't haul a loaded beer-wagon, or a Clydesdale because it can't do sixteen furlongs in a minute and a half. Best-quality English guns are built to achieve maximum strength at minimum weight for specific purposes, and they're built to do their jobs with ammunition loaded to certain mean working pressures. In other words, you can't stuff just any cartridges into just any English gun and expect them to be compatible.

Pigeon and wildfowl guns are built specifically for a diet of heavy loads; standard game guns are not, and too many heavy loads will literally pound one to death. It has nothing to do with sidelock or boxlock or intrinsic quality, only with ignorance.

If some of the presumptions about sidelock guns don't hold up in the face of fact, many of those brought to bear against boxlocks don't either. Most American boxlocks are too heavy, but that's the other side of the reason why English sidelock game guns can't hack a lifetime of super-duper magnum loads. American guns are built to take anything, or at least anything available at the time they were made. Parker is the worst offender in this; a Parker is hell for stout, but it also can feel like a bois d'arc fencepost by the end of the day. As a rule, Fox guns are the lightest among American pieces, and you can find boxlocks built elsewhere that are as light and lithe as any sidelock.

Not all boxlocks have bad triggers either. Some do, but then so do some sidelocks. Less-expensive guns tend to have the roughest, hardest trigger pulls—not because they're boxlocks but rather because they weren't treated to much handwork when they were built. If sidelocks have any advantage on this account it's that their triggers are a bit easier to adjust, since the sears are easier to get at, but that doesn't mean boxlock triggers can't be just as good.

Intercepting or safety sears are one point where most sidelocks truly can claim superiority over most boxlocks. Interceptors are secondary sears that prevent a sidelock's tumbler from falling if the main sear is tripped by anything other than the trigger—by, say, the gun being dropped or by recoil from the first shot—and they've been standard equipment in better sidelocks for a hundred years. It's possible to devise interceptors for boxlocks but not at all easy, and very few boxlocks have ever had them. None of the great American guns did, not even the L.C. Smith. (No doubt L.C. Smith, and later the Hunter brothers, chose not to use interceptors as one way of keeping prices for Smith guns in line with the prices of their boxlock competitors—which illustrates just how difficult, if not impossible, it is to build sidelocks and boxlocks of equal quality at equal cost.)

Sidelocks also have an edge on emergency repairs. If you have to, and if you have the spare parts, you can replace a sidelock main or sear spring in the field with a screwdriver and pliers. Doing similar work on most boxlocks requires much more work and a fair supply of tools besides. The most famous and, for all I know, the only exception is the Westley Richards droplock—a boxlock whose locks can be changed in a matter of seconds, thanks to a design patented by John Deeley and Leslie Taylor in 1897.

The concepts of beauty and grace are so thoroughly mixed up with the vagaries of personal taste that they're scarcely worth getting into. But we're here, so what the hell. So long as it's clear that I'm talking about my taste. Yours may be different. I'm also talking about pure form, not decoration.

To my eyes, nothing in the world is lovelier than a fine sidelock gun in the traditional London mold—and that includes Candice Bergen and Mary McDonnell (*Dances With Wolves* is pleasant viewing for more than just the scenery). A fine boxlock isn't far behind, but boxlocks are problematic, mainly because they come in so many shapes and forms. Some are so square and boxy as to be just plain ugly. Others—Westley Richards, for instance—are still basically square and boxy, but something about them lends genuine beauty. Parkers are extremely handsome guns. Foxes strike me as the most elegantly beautiful of all.

The line where a boxlock frame meets the stock is a problem because it runs counter to all the other lines of the gun. Makers have tried all sorts of ways to soften the visual blow, most successfully by filing scallops into the frame, creating what the Birmingham trade calls a "fancy back." Decorative, non-functional sideplates often solve the problem and provide good surfaces for engraving besides. They're fine so long as the rest of the gun is gracefully shaped. Francotte uses false plates particularly well. Stock panels carved to a sidelock shape and finished with graceful points are nice, too—although less so, to my eye, if they're checkered.

About the most you can say is that such matters are purely personal taste, answerable to neither rhyme nor reason. Which is good, because this would be a dull business if all guns looked the same.

When you come right down to it, the most compelling difference between a sidelock and a boxlock is the price tag. Dollar for dollar a boxlock almost always represents more gun for the money. There are some exceptions, but not many. If you like sidelocks and can afford the extra bucks, by all means have one. If not, there's a whole world of splendid boxlocks to choose among. It's been my experience that a monstrous horrendum can make a wonderfully faithful friend.

18

Safety Systems

Historically, the first order of business among gunmakers has been, as Tom Purdey once remarked, "to make the bloody thing go 'bang.'" That was the main intent behind the first mechanical gunlock, created in the mid-fifteenth century, and the same notion has for the most part continued to define the gunmaker's efforts ever since. But the evolution of the gun, like that of a living organism, has steadily worked to unify a complex range of functions, some of them seemingly contradictory, and it wasn't long before makers came to realize a certain merit in finding ways to make the bloody thing *not* go "bang."

We tend to think of safety systems as unique to hammerless guns, but they aren't. No one knows who first conceived a mechanism for preventing a gun from firing accidentally nor when such a device was first installed, but we do know that it happened early on. Even the wheellock, developed in Europe early in the sixteenth century, included a safety of sorts; the dog-head—which held a chunk of iron pyrite against a spring-loaded wheel to produce a spark—was mounted on a pivot so it could be kept out of contact with the wheel until the shooter wanted the gun to fire.

A more sophisticated safety feature appeared during the next phase of evolution. One major difference between the wheellock and its successor, the flintlock, is that the mainspring was attached to the dog-head, thereby creating what we now recognize as a hammer. The earliest English version of the flintlock, invented about 1600 and commonly called the dog lock, featured a pivoting hook or "dog," fastened to the outside of the lockplate, that securely held the hammer halfway between full cock and fully forward. Eventually, some gunmaker simplified the concept by adding a second notch to the tumbler—the internal lock part to which the hammer is attached—so that the sear itself could hold the hammer at half-cock.

It was an excellent idea, and it probably did make a gun safer from accidental firing, particularly since the second notch generally was quite deep. But though the half-cock principle remains a standard feature of exposed-hammer guns even today, it clearly wasn't the ultimate answer. Otherwise, "going off half-cocked" wouldn't still be part of everyday language.

Around the turn of the nineteenth century, Joseph Manton, the first truly great English gunmaker and the man who virtually defined the sporting gun as we now know it, concluded that guns could be made safer by blocking both hammers and triggers. For the hammers, Manton designed and patented a device he called a gravitational stop, a free-pivoting steel toggle pinned to the outside of the lockplate. When the gun is held with the muzzles up, the stops drop back under their own weight and block the hammers, preventing them from falling if the shooter got too enthusiastic with the ramrod and jarred the gun off half-cock while seating wads.

Though effective, Manton's gravitational stops never became standard fare among English guns, in part because they worked only when the gun was vertical and in part because muzzleloading guns were on the verge of obsolescence by the time the patent expired. The trigger-block system, though, was more enduring.

Joseph Manton is generally credited with inventing the grip safety, a concept widely used among shotguns throughout the nineteenth century, occasionally in the twentieth century, and one still used in certain handguns. Manton's design involved a trigger-block linked mechanically to a lever in the stock wrist, and the triggers were free to move only when the shooter held the lever down. Theoretically the gun was capable of firing only when held in firing position. But as Greener later pointed out, a gun often is held by the wrist when it's being carried, so the grip safety that places the lever on the underside of the wrist behind the trigger guard is likely to be deactivated most of the time the gun is in someone's hands.

Such objections aside, grip safeties were enormously popular in England, with at least fourteen different designs patented between 1855 and 1865. Some were operated by a lever or button placed at the top or side of the wrist; these presumably were less likely to be disengaged while the gun was carried. Some of the more freewheeling minds came up with variations on the grip-safety theme and put the release lever in the buttplate so that the safety disengaged when the shooter shouldered the gun. Greener designed a butt safety in 1879; S.W. Silver, inventor of the famous Silver's recoil pad, designed a similar device in the 1880s.

Virtually all of the early safety systems that acted directly upon the hammers were meant to secure them at full cock. A number of later ones, developed both in England and on the Continent and adapted to the rebounding locks perfected by John Stanton in 1869, did just the opposite. These, usually by means of sliding or pivoting catches on the lockplates, blocked the hammers in the rebound position so they couldn't accidentally be knocked against the firing pins.

The hammerless action, which came to full flower in the 1870s, made some sort of reliable safety device a necessity.

Early versions, cocked by an external lever, shared one of the most serious of the hammer gun's hazards—the perennial danger of the hammer-spur or cocking lever slipping out of the shooter's hand before the sears engaged. Under a strong mainspring, a hammer dropped even short of half-cock could hit hard enough to fire the gun, and one that slipped just before full cock could break the half-cock notch. As a boy, my father endured the horror of watching his cousin die from a gunshot inflicted by a third youngster on a rabbit-hunting trip, and it happened just that way. Slip-fires aren't unheard-of even now.

Even the earliest lever-cocking hammerless actions—Theophilus Murcott's, patented in 1871, and Gibbs and Pitt's, patented in 1873—contained some sort of mechanical safety. Murcott's blocked the triggers and was operated by a small lever fastened to the top tang. Gibbs and Pitt designed a safety that blocked the tumblers and put the catch on the right-hand side of the frame.

Hammerless actions of the sort invented by Anson and Deeley in 1875, cocked internally by leverage from the barrels, generally don't suffer the problem of slip-firing, but unlike a hammer gun or a lever-cocker, you can't carry one loaded and uncocked, so it has to have a safety of some sort. The earliest Anson and Deeley design included what amounts to the typical double-gun safety of today: a trigger-block connected to a sliding button mounted on the top tang. William Anson seems to have taken a particular interest in safety systems and continued tinkering with different designs for several years, but for the most part the original Anson and Deeley concept remains the world standard.

Not that other systems lacked virtue. In February 1879, Joseph Needham and George Hinton received a British patent for a what commonly is called the intercepting safety or safety sear. This device is meant to lock the tumbler itself so that the gun won't fire if the sear is jarred loose by some accident. It's meant to disengage when the trigger is pulled and to act independently of the trigger-block safety. The idea wasn't a new one, but the Needham and Hinton mechanism was original enough to satisfy both the British and American patent offices, and an American patent was issued March 30, 1880.

Needham and Hinton assigned ownership of the design to William and James Scott, gunmakers, of Birmingham, and the device was for many years known as the Scott safety. Other makers contrived their own means of accomplishing the same thing. Holland & Holland's version, like Needham and Hinton's, is made for sidelock guns; W.W. Greener, S.W. Silver, and others successfully applied the notion to boxlocks.

Trying to improve upon the simple, tang-mounted, trigger-block safety seems to have preoccupied some clever people on both sides of the Atlantic. Greener liked the trigger-block but insisted on putting the button on the left side of the gun, an arrangement that became something of a Greener signature. It's also a damnably inconvenient place for a safety button. Around the turn of the century Charles Addison Young, an American trapshooter, devised a curious safety device as an option for his sliding-barrel repeater; disengaging the safety requires a backward pull of about four pounds' pressure on the fore-end. Young later designed and patented a grip and a butt safety. None caught the American shooter's fancy. Except for Greener's, the typical English game gun has a safety button on the tang.

Actually, about the only really ingenious work on safeties to come along in a hundred years are the various ways in which barrel selectors for single triggers have been incorporated with safety buttons. In one of Dan Lefever's designs, pushing the safety forward sets the trigger to fire the right barrel first; pulling it back establishes a left-right sequence. Browning's safety button/barrel selector moves from side to side as well as back and forth. Winchester, Remington, Ruger, Beretta, and a world of others have all composed variations on the same theme.

So how safe is any of them? There seems no doubt that an intercepting sear in combination with a trigger-block offers about as much mechanical safety as could reasonably be built into a gun. But intercepting safeties are tricky to properly make and adjust, and you seldom find one on anything other than an extremely expensive piece. (Ruger's Red Label over-under, fitted with what Ruger calls a "hammer interrupter," is a notable exception.) None of the great old American doubles had them. Whether any gun needs one is debatable. Greener argues that an intercepting safety is of real value only in an ejector gun—because mistimed ejectors can fool the shooter into believing the locks are cocked when they aren't and can lead to the hammerless gun's equivalent of the slip-fire. Maybe so, though I've used some guns with ejectors that worked about as badly as ejectors can work, and I've never had that problem.

More to the point, a well-designed, well-made sear isn't as liable to being jarred loose as it might seem, particularly that of a hammerless lock, which doesn't have any external action parts to get knocked around. The same applies to repeaters, which traditionally are fitted only with trigger-block safeties.

No mechanical device, alone or in combination, is any kind of substitute for safe gun handling. A positive trigger-block is to my mind a necessity on any gun other than a highly specialized target piece. An intercepting safety is a nice refinement for a game gun, but you can accomplish the same end in a better way by never allowing the gun out of your hands unless it's unloaded or the action is open. And in any case, it's where you point the muzzles that counts.

19

The Electric Gun

Igniting a charge of powder with a bit of fire is one of the elemental concepts of the gun, a dualistic notion that combines to create the fire in firearm. Some sort of propellent has to burn and something has to start it burning—whether it's a flaming stick, a smoldering length of tow, sparks from a chunk of pyrite or flint, or a tiny chemical explosion.

As early as the mid-sixteenth century, European alchemists knew that certain chemicals, notably various salts of fulminic acid, are highly explosive. Alexander Forsyth discovered in 1807 that a pellet of fulminate struck by a hammer produces a spark sufficient to ignite gunpowder, and thereby set the course that the development of primers has followed ever since. Subsequent efforts have focused almost exclusively upon making chemically explosive primers more efficient.

But every field has a share of freewheeling types inclined to think outside the nine dots, so to speak, and a few have experimented with other ways of setting off a powder charge. Inevitably, some have tried electricity.

The earliest attempts date almost to the time we first learned to produce electric current by chemical reaction. Greener describes a muzzleloader built in Czechoslovakia about 1870 with a dichromate battery and induction coil fitted into an iron buttstock. A button, located where the trigger normally would be, activates a series of spring-driven rods and cams to close a circuit and deliver a spark to the chamber.

The 1880s saw a small flurry of patents covering electrical-ignition systems. In England, Frederick Bertie Worsley Roberts and Benjamin Theophilus Moore jointly earned one in 1882, as did Nelson Goodwin Green, followed in 1884 by Thomas Page-Wood and John Andrews.

In 1883 the great Belgian gunmaker Henri Pieper developed an electrically primed breechloader powered by a battery in the shooter's pocket. The battery, or "accumulator," as Pieper called it, was wired to a contact in a pad the shooter wore on his shoulder, and a metal buttplate on the gun provided the other contact.

American inventors were even busier. Dr. Samuel Russell, a physician in Brooklyn, New York, earned three separate patents for electric guns—one in October 1884 and two in March 1886—and assigned them all to the American Electric Arms & Ammunition Company of New York City. In July 1887 Edgar A. Monfort also received patent protection for an electrical breechloader, which he assigned to the Universal Electric Arms & Ammunition Company, also of New York City. The location and similarity of names leads me to wonder if American and Universal weren't in fact the same company. But I don't know for sure.

I do know that on August 27, 1883, Alexander T. Brown of Syracuse, New York, filed application to patent an electrically fired shotgun. Like Henri Pieper, Brown was no slouch at designing guns. Six months earlier he had applied for patents on what would be the L.C. Smith hammer gun, and two years later he would design the classic Smith hammerless gun.

Brown's patent, which was issued January 1, 1884, specifies a gun fitted with "an induction-coil in conjunction with any suitable electric generator, whereby connections may be made from the coil to the cartridge, and the powder in the cartridge ignited by means of a spark." The design is simple enough, with a pair of wires from the trigger to the primary coil and another pair from the secondary coil to the cartridge. One of these two wires runs from the coil to the safety, the other from the coil through the standing breech, where it acts as a contact with the cartridge. The trigger, to all appearances a conventional shotgun trigger, acts as a switch to close the circuit.

The most interesting feature is Brown's adaptation of a typical tang-mounted button to serve as a safety device in the electrical circuit. In the forward or safe position the button leaves a gap in the wires from the secondary coil to the cartridge. Pulled back, it contacts a wire from the coil and completes the secondary circuit through the steel frame of the gun. Presumably, the trigger and safety could perform identical functions so that one could hold back the trigger with the safety on and fire the gun by closing the circuit with the safety button.

In all, Brown was awarded patent protection on six different features of the design. He assigned half-ownership to his employer, Lyman C. Smith, and the two may have considered manufacturing the gun under the L.C. Smith name. If so, it was a passing fancy, for Alexander Brown's electric shotgun never was put into production. In fact, scarcely any of the systems patented here or in Europe actually amounted to anything more than drawings and paperwork.

The military has been most successful at finding practical uses for electric guns. At the end of World War II, the U.S. Air Force converted its twin 20 mm aircraft cannon to electric ignition. Even the best mechanical triggers usually allowed one cannon to fire a few milliseconds ahead of the other, and recoil from the first deflected the aim of the second. Electric ignition provided a way to fire both guns at precisely the same instant.

Electric game guns have proven far less practical, and none has been manufactured in quantity anywhere in the world. For a while in the 1960s a French firm called Rouby built an electric double gun powered by a battery pack in the buttstock, but like all the rest it made no impression on the market.

The problem with an electric gun is that it has to have electric ammunition, and no one has yet figured out how to manufacture electric cartridges that can sell at reasonable prices.

There are two basic types of electric primers. One uses a priming mixture that conducts electric current but with a relatively high resistance. An electrode in the shell head, placed where a conventional primer normally is, extends into this mixture and sends electricity from the power source into the priming mix. As the current passes through the mix the resistance generates sufficient heat to ignite the primer. Naturally the priming compound has to be formulated just right, but when it is the system works quite well, especially for 20 mm military shells.

The other system is what David Butler calls the bridgewire primer. Here, an insulated conductor in the center of the cartridge head is grounded by fine wires to the outer cup of the primer assembly—or to the shell head itself, in the case of Henri Pieper's cartridge. These heat quickly as current passes through them, thereby igniting the priming mixture. Alexander Brown's cartridge worked on the same principle, and the Rouby shells used fine Nichrome wires. This system, too, functions well for military ammunition.

The obvious advantage of electric ignition is that it reduces lock time—the six to ten milliseconds between the time you pull the trigger and the time the gun actually fires—simply because an electric current moves faster than the mechanism of a gun lock. Since the trigger is nothing more than a switch, its pull can be extremely short and light. This may be significant for ultra-refined match rifles and pistols or for a target gun in the hands of a world-class shot, but a millisecond or two more or less hardly matters in a game gun.

Given current technology, building a good electric gun wouldn't be difficult at all, probably easier than building one of the conventional type. Having reliable, low-cost ammunition to go with it is the catch since neither of the two basic priming systems is wholly suitable. The bridge-wire type is the most useful for small arms since it will work at the low voltage levels that small batteries deliver—but hand-soldering hairlike wires into every primer is not the route to manufacturing economy. If we're to have good electric cartridges, someone will once again have to think outside the nine dots.

Still, at a time when printed circuitry and microchips can do everything from rendering these words onto my computer screen to sending a thirty-five-year-old Miles Davis recording to the speakers in the next room, who knows what's coming next?

Part II

SHOOTING

CRAFT, CARTRIDGES, AND CONTROVERSIES

CRAFT

20

Eyes

Intercepting a moving object with a charge of shot is a matter of coordination between eyes and hands. You can't hit what you can't see, except by accident, and all the visual acuity of a Cooper's hawk won't do you the slightest good unless your hands move the gun to where your eyes say it ought to be.

Fortunately, we have a splendid computer between our ears, a control center capable of sorting out highly complicated eye-hand interactions without any conscious direction other than an initial decision to do this or that—whether it's picking up a pencil, tying your boots, playing a Beethoven sonata, or hitting a tennis ball with a racket or a quail with a load of 9s. Practice enough to develop some kinetic memory, and your brain takes over from there.

Seems simple enough, and in fact, it is. Except when it isn't. The human brain is a wondrous thing, but like any computer, its ability to function depends upon how accurately the circuits are wired, how straightforward the programming, how clever the operator. In shooting, as in similar tasks, the key is to understand how your own computer works and then find ways of helping it do its thing with the least amount of conscious interference on your part.

Every normally functioning brain coordinates eyes and hands with great finesse, but it favors one eye and one hand over the other. Just as the majority of us are either right- or left-handed, so are we either right- or left-eyed, and the dominant eye and hand are usually on the same side. When they aren't—when, for instance, a right-handed person's left eye is the master—the phenomenon is called cross-dominance. You can live a whole lifetime without ever knowing you're cross-dominant or noticing any handicap from it—until you try shooting a shotgun.

A shotgunner gains a distinct advantage from shooting with both eyes open, but the eye on the same side as the shoulder you shoot from needs to be in control if the gun is to truly point where you look. If you're same-side dominant and want to see why a cross-dominant person has a hard time, shoulder your gun, point it at some small object across the room, and close the eye nearest the gunstock—your right eye, in other words, if the gun is at your right shoulder.

The first thing you notice is that the gun appears to be pointing to the right of whatever you sighted on. Still keeping your right eye closed, reposition the gun so the bead is on the object, then open your right eye. You'll find that the gun actually is pointing well to the left, which is exactly where you'd shoot if the object were a straightaway target, because you naturally point where your dominant eye says to.

Cross-dominance can be enormously frustrating. A left-eyed right-hander tends to hit right-to-left angling targets fairly well, because the master left eye builds in some unconscious lead. But he'll consistently shoot behind anything angling from left to right and will nearly always miss straightaways because he shoots to the left. A right-eyed left-hander has the same problems, only in reverse.

There are several ways to learn which is your dominant eye, if you don't already know. The simplest is to extend your dominant hand full length and with both eyes open, point your index finger at something; then close the eye opposite your dominant hand. If your finger still appears to point at the same spot, you probably are same-side dominant. Now close the eye on the same side as your dominant hand and you should see the object off to the side of your finger. If you can't tell much difference, point at something farther away. The greater the distance, the greater the discrepancy will appear.

If you still can't see a difference, you might have what's known as central vision, which means that neither eye is truly dominant. Its effect on shooting is much the same as cross-dominance, although usually not as pronounced. It also lends a baffling inconsistency, though, because one eye or the other sometimes takes over, and you can't know from shot to shot which it will be. True central vision is uncommon but certainly not unheard-of. I have one close friend who's central-sighted, and I've discovered the phenomenon in two of my shooting students over the years.

Cross-dominance, on the other hand, is quite common, and in my experience, it's somewhat more prevalent among women than among men. I don't know why that should be, but I do know that fully half the women I've taught to shoot, my wife included, are cross-dominant. If I had to hazard a guess, I'd say it has something to do with the corpus callosum, the main bundle of nerves connecting the right and left hemispheres of our brains. Transmission of nerve impulses through the system may be slightly more active or more efficient in women. This is purely speculation, so if you know of any research that sheds some light on this, I'd be interested to hear of it.

At any rate, if you're coaching a beginning shooter, child or adult, the first thing to do is determine which eye is dominant—particularly if you're working with your wife, daughter, or girlfriend. Regardless of sex, don't simply assume same-side dominance, because it'll be a frustrating experience for you both if you're wrong. It's not a bad idea to check your own master eye now and then, even if you're a veteran shooter. One eye may not be as strongly dominant as you think, and besides, eyes change as we grow older. I know a couple of cross-dominant shooters who weren't that way in younger years, and one of my friends has a left eye that tends to take over when he begins to tire. The better you know what's going on, the better able you are to do something about it.

Cross-dominance usually is easy to diagnose. Central vision is more difficult. If the finger-pointing test seems inconclusive or inconsistent, go to the gun itself. Shoulder it first on the same side as your dominant hand, sight on some distant mark, and close the opposite eye; then switch the gun to the other shoulder and do the same thing. A person of true central vision can sight with equal accuracy from either shoulder with both eyes open.

Either way, cross-dominance or central vision, you have some options in how you deal with the problem. Cross-dominant people can switch sides and shoot from the shoulder corresponding to the dominant eye, but that's difficult for most of us because we're decidedly right- or left-handed and it takes a long time to get used to shooting the other way around. Some never do.

A cross-over or cross-eyed stock also is a possibility. This allows you to shoulder the gun with your dominant hand but brings the rib in line with the opposite eye. The same concept, with slightly less bend, works for someone with central vision by centering the rib so he can look down it with both eyes. Cross-over stocks look a bit weird, but they work, and they're probably the best choice of all for a shooter who has lost most or all vision in the eye on his dominant-hand side. Those blind in one eye from birth can readily learn to shoot from the opposite shoulder; one of my gunning partners did just that. He does everything right-handed except shoot, and he's a first-class game shot. It isn't so easy for someone who has lost sight later and has to relearn how to handle a gun.

A cross-dominant or central-sighted shooter can adopt Robert Churchill's advice and hold the gunbarrels with the thumb blocking the line of sight from the opposite eye, but it doesn't work well, if at all, with any gun but a side-by-side. Or you can simply close one eye when you shoot. It works, but you lose half your peripheral vision and much of your ability to judge distance and angle. As a better solution, you can stick a small patch of tape on the lens of your shooting glasses, placed precisely where it masks the muzzle and front bead from your off eye. That way, you still retain full peripheral vision, and the patch seems to do less mischief to your depth perception.

For shooting skeet and trap, the patch needn't be large, less than the diameter of a dime, in fact. For sporting clays and game shooting, where targets appear at a greater variety of heights and angles, a narrow strip of tape placed vertically across the lens will prevent you from peeking under the mask on high incoming shots; when that happens, your dominant eye instantly takes control and your shot charge goes awry.

If you're same-side dominant but not strongly so, or if your master eye loses its dominance with fatigue, an old target-shooter's trick comes in handy: when your off eye starts taking over, rub a fingertip on your nose or forehead to pick up some skin oil, and make a little smudge on your glasses in the same place where you'd put a patch of tape. A spot of lip-balm or bit of spit and dust works, too—as will anything that blurs or blocks the vision in the eye that's not supposed to be governing where you shoot.

Eyes are splendidly precise instruments without which there'd be no shooting, good or bad.

21

Hands

I suggested in the last chapter that precise coordination between eyes and hands is the essence of successful shooting. Both have certain tasks to perform in aid of placing a shot charge on a moving target, and both tasks are vitally important.

Eyes are navigators. Their job is to calculate where a gunbarrel needs to be in relation to the target. Hands are responsible for getting it there and keeping it on course. Hands are the pilots, and where they go, so goes the shot.

Those who for some reason lack vision in one eye or the use of one hand certainly can learn to shoot and shoot well. But for the sake of discussing the concept, let's assume that the average shooter is equipped with two eyes and two hands, all fully functional.

As I said in the last chapter, most of us have one eye that dominates the other. The master eye acts as the chief navigator and the other as an assistant. The subordinate eye broadens our field of peripheral vision and allows us to judge distance and angle, but the dominant one ultimately decides what message is sent to the brain.

We also have a dominant hand, one we instinctively use first and use to perform tasks that require the greatest precision and complexity. Unlike eyes, the subordinate hand is not simply an adjunct to the other; instead, it can perform precise, complex tasks of its own, separately and yet in perfect coordination with the other. If this weren't so, we'd never be able to play musical instruments, type, juggle, or do dozens of other uniquely human things.

Wingshooting also is a two-handed affair, requiring close coordination. A shooter's hands move the gun from some starting position into shooting position, guide the barrels along the path determined by the eyes, press the trigger in response to a command issued by the brain. Eyes and brain create and direct the intention, but hands perform the act.

Even though shooting is, or should be, a function of the entire body, hands are in many ways the essence of technique, and different shooting methods ask different things of a shooter's hands.

One school of thought favors giving the trigger hand a high degree of control over the barrels, arguing that the dominant hand should play a dominant role in swinging the gun. This is essentially an American notion, based on rifle shooting, and it explains why Americans are so fond of full-pistol-grip stocks. The more wood you give the trigger hand to hold onto, the firmer grasp it has and therefore the more it can influence gun movement.

Trapshooters like this idea especially well. For one thing, it's nicely suited to the game. All the shots are at going-away targets, and a quick gunner seldom has to move his muzzle more than about a foot in any direction. Add in the rule that allows the shooter to shoulder his gun and snuggle comfortably around it before he calls for the target, and the sum of it all is that American-style trap encourages more riflelike shooting than any other shotgun game. Targets are small, and precision is important.

Having the trigger hand in control of the gun helps provide that precision. It helps dampen recoil as well, and recoil is the nemesis of every serious trapshooter. Look around at any trap tournament, and you'll see pistol grips galore, in every style from factory standard to wildly exaggerated. You'll find much the same on skeet ranges, too, for essentially the same reasons.

But game-shooting needn't be so precise, and the technique that works in shooting targets with a premounted gun doesn't translate very well into the field, where distances vary and angles come in literally infinite variety. You can't memorize the shots that game birds present, and they seldom give you time to adjust and readjust the gun against your shoulder and cheek, so you need a well-fitted stock and a highly adaptable technique, an efficient, economical set of movements you can perform without wasting time or motion. This, if it's to be successful, requires an altogether different way of using your hands.

The British have more thoroughly refined the art of wingshooting than anyone on earth, mainly because they've been at it longer and have taken it more seriously than anyone else. In the British approach, your forward hand is the key. Your forward hand holds the barrels and moves them where your eyes say they should go. Your other hand follows and triggers the shot at the proper moment.

It's as simple as that—in concept, anyway. It's also enormously effective, because it takes full advantage of our brains' natural ability to coordinate our eyes and hands. You don't even need a gun to see how it works. Next time you see a bird, any bird, on the wing, point to it with your left hand, and then think about what you did. Chances are, you extended your arm straight out, or nearly so, lined up your index finger with your master eye, and swept it precisely along the bird's line of flight. And you did it all instinctively, in a matter of milliseconds, with no more conscious effort than making the decision to point in the first place. That's how our brains work.

Thinking of the gun barrel as an extension of the forward hand is central to the British approach. If you search long enough, you can find a hundred or more different shooting methods currently taught in Britain, but for the most part, they're more alike than different. Nearly all, whether espoused by disciples of Churchill, Stanbury, or someone else, agree that the forward hand is the one that truly controls the shot.

Although the concept makes perfect sense, it also creates something of a paradox, because to an extent it works against our natural tendency to use our dominant hand first, and instead requires the subordinate hand to take the leading role in a fairly complex maneuver. This is why the classic English game gun has a straight-hand stock—not because it's aesthetically more pleasing nor because British stockmakers don't know how to carve pistol grips, and certainly not to allow you to slide your hand backward to pull the second trigger.

A straight-hand stock is a deliberate means of diminishing the dominant hand's ability to overpower the other. It simply offers less to hold onto. You can't grasp it very firmly, especially with your ring and little fingers, without cocking your wrist at an uncomfortable angle. But this is okay, because you don't need to have a death grip on the gun with either hand, and especially not with the trigger hand. All that hand needs to do is help lift the gun and then press the trigger, and it can do both those things best when it's relatively relaxed.

A straight grip also makes a subtle difference in how you mount the gun, again because of the angle at which it places your wrist. It prompts you to raise your elbow a wee bit higher than a pistol-grip stock does. This means you're more likely to bring the gun up to your cheek instead of lowering your head to meet the stock—which in turn means you're less likely to raise your head off the stock at the critical moment.

For all the good things it contributes to successful shooting, a straight grip has one disadvantage, or at least a potential disadvantage. Recoil sometimes can drive the gun backwards with enough force that it slips through the trigger hand and raps the trigger-guard smartly against the second finger. This can be surprisingly painful, even with light loads, and it's a quick way to develop a big-time flinch. It probably happens most often with straight-gripped guns, but it can happen with a half-hand or half-pistol grip, too.

You can buy a little rubber cushion that clips onto the trigger-guard, but the proper solution depends upon whether the problem is chronic or occasional. Chronic cases typically involve a double-triggered gun and a shooter who has unusually small hands or short fingers. He has to crowd his hand against the guard in order to reach the front trigger and therefore gets smacked more or less soundly every time he fires the right barrel. He'd be better off with a single trigger, placed well back in the guard.

A stock that's too short can have much the same effect. The shooter unconsciously pushes the gun forward to create a comfortable distance between his nose and his trigger hand, thereby creating an equal gap between the butt and his shoulder. The gun jumps back under recoil, slips through his hands, and bangs his shoulder and finger at about the same time.

Even a perfectly fitted gun occasionally will bruise a finger. In those cases the culprit invariably is an error in timing or grip—either in triggering the shot before you get the butt against your shoulder or in taking too loose a grasp with your forward hand. The forward hand is not only best able to control the barrels but also is best able to absorb recoil, particularly if you shoot with your arm well extended. You don't need to squeeze so hard that your knuckles turn pale, but you do need to have a reasonably firm hold on the business end—both to hit the target and to keep the gun from hitting you.

Actually, a rap on the hand now and then isn't necessarily a bad deal, because it's an effective admonition against letting your technique get sloppy. When it happens to me, I always remember a teacher I had years ago, a forthright lady of advancing years who liked to deal with momentary lapses of behavior in her students by administering a wooden ruler across the back of the hand. Not fun, mind you, but it does keep you on your toes.

22

Technique

I'm not sure I remember this exactly the way I first heard it, but as I recall, two grouse hunters were talking about the tribulations of getting lost. One told a long, harrowing tale of spending two nights in the woods, walking at least forty miles before finding his way out, and wound it up by declaring that he had carried a compass ever since.

"Never owned one," the other said.

"What do you do if you get lost?"

"Nothing to it. I just fire twice, yell 'How in the hell could I miss that shot?'—and three guys come out of the bushes to tell me what I did wrong. One of 'em always knows the way back to the road."

Well, I don't know why you missed your last shot, or even *if* you did. But we've got a few minutes before the other two guys show up, so I'll tell you some things that a lot of shooters do wrong. And suggest some things that might help you hit your next shot.

In the past two chapters, I've talked about shooting as an exercise in hand-eye coordination and focused at some length on the two main components. Eyes have a certain job to do, and so do hands—the trick is getting them to work together in consistent, useful ways. Look around long enough and you'll find any number of prescriptions for accomplishing just that, shooting methods by the dozen, each one established by some particularly skillful shot, each with its coterie of disciples. On a close look, you'll find that a lot of them directly contradict a lot of others.

Arguably, results are the ultimate measure of technique; if you can hit a clay target or a game bird, who's to say you went about it the wrong way? But what if you can't, or can't hit them consistently? What if there's a certain shot you don't hit at all, an angle so baffling that you've given up trying? Seems to me the ultimate measures of technique ought to be adaptability and consistency. And simplicity as well.

The fundamental flaw in a great many prescriptions is that they seek to stuff every shooter into a single mold, based on the proposition that if I'm a great shot, you can be a great shot, too, provided you do exactly as I do. Or vice versa. The problem is that we're all different, and the more complicated a method becomes, the less able it is to accommodate the differences. What works for one might work for another up to a point, but beyond that, attempting to copy someone else down to the last detail usually is a ticket to frustration.

Better to take a simpler approach, to toss out everything that has to do with individual differences in physique, reflexes, temperament, and the rest; to concentrate instead on making best use of the one gift we all have—a brain naturally designed to coordinate our eyes and hands with remarkable precision.

Think of it as a computer. Press the right button and it does what it's programmed to do, without any further direction. Programming, of course, is crucial, because like any computer, the brain operates according to the rule of garbage in, garbage out. Put the right things in, and you'll get the right things out. I've spent nearly a lifetime searching for good things to put in, sorting through one technique after another, winnowing bits and pieces from mountains of chaff, but it didn't really come together until a few years ago, when I met Jack Mitchell.

My friend Jack is a puckish Englishman who's spent a lifetime in the shooting trade, with Cogswell & Harrison and as chief instructor at the West London Shooting Grounds. Now he makes twice-yearly tours through the United States, booking American gunners to shoot driven pheasants in England and teaching us how to hit them.

The important thing is that Jack Mitchell owns a rare and lovely gift: he is a superb teacher, the best I've ever met—and I've met a lot of them, either in person, on film, or in print. No approach I know makes more sense. It's brilliantly simple, adaptable to any shooter and any target at any angle or speed, and it's based wholly on the hand-eye coordination built into us all.

In the last chapter I suggested a little exercise of pointing at a passing bird to illustrate how we're able to accurately pick up a moving object's line of flight without much conscious effort. You can do the same with a gunbarrel in your hand, and if you think of the barrel as a literal extension of your arm, you're well on the right track. I suggest to my students that they imagine the barrel is a brush with which they're going to paint a stripe along the target's path and right on through the middle of it.

To get the best feel for this, it helps to take a fairly long hold on the gun with your forward hand, to extend your hand as you would if you were pointing your finger. You can even extend your index finger along the underside of the barrels.

Since Jack emphasizes moving the barrel along the target's flight path, you could accurately call it a swing-through approach. Spot- and sustained-lead shooting are okay for trap and skeet, but swinging through is the easiest way to consistently hit game birds and sporting clays targets, because it accomplishes several things at once. For one, it gets you instantly onto the proper angle, simply because you're moving the barrels from where the target was, to where it is, to where it will be when the shot charge gets there. For another, swinging through establishes lead automatically; if you start from behind, you have to move the barrels faster than the target's flying in order to catch it, and so long as you don't slow down or stop when you do catch up, simple inertia builds in some forward allowance.

If you spend some time watching people shoot, you'll notice that most handle a shotgun as if it were a rifle: slam the stock to the shoulder with the trigger hand, lower the cheek to the comb, get locked onto the gun, raise the barrel, and then start hurrying after the target.

This creates several problems. Raising the butt causes the muzzle to dip, which means you're starting well below the flight line rather than on it. Mounting the gun before starting the swing distracts your attention from the target, just when you should be reading the flight path. It also turns your upper body into a turret flexible in all directions, and that makes straying above or below the flight path all the more likely as you rush to catch up with a target that's fast escaping.

Jack Mitchell's way is better. As he puts it: Move your forward hand before you move your trigger hand, and don't move your head at all. In other words, combine the swing and mount into a single motion, and bring the stock up to your face instead of lowering your face to the stock. It's a wonderfully economical movement and perfectly easy to do once you get the idea.

The first step is the ready position, with the barrels pointed about where you expect the target to appear and the butt tucked underneath your armpit, just far enough so you can't lift it without snagging. This helps prevent your trigger hand from sneaking in too soon. You can even begin this way in a lot of field-shooting situations.

When a target appears, the first thing to do is watch it, to identify its line of flight. Don't move the gun at all until you know where the target's going, because if you don't know that, you might as well not shoot. Don't panic; you have more time than you think.

The first move is to push the muzzles toward the target with your forward hand, into line with your master eye and onto the target's flight path. You're actually beginning the swing right now, with the first movement. This initial push forward brings the butt clear of your armpit and allows the trigger hand to follow where your forward hand leads.

Accelerate the muzzles after the target with your forward hand, as if you were going to point your finger at it, paint a stripe through it, trace its path with a pencil—whatever metaphor helps you visualize the process. Keep lifting the gun all the while, bringing the stock toward your shoulder and cheek, bringing the plane of the barrels into line with your eyes.

Ideally, the stock should touch your shoulder and cheek simultaneously, at about the same time the muzzles catch up with the target. Do not, at this point, lock onto the gun and continue to ride it. You don't have to; if the muzzles have come along the target's line of flight, moving faster than the target is, and if the gun fits properly so that you're looking right down the rib, all you have to do is pull the trigger and it's dead.

By all means, do not stop to think about lead. On quartering and other shallow-angle shots, you needn't be aware of lead at all. Fire as soon as you catch the target, as if you're going to shoot right at it; the momentum of your swing will take care of what little lead is required. Longer, crossing shots do require substantial forward allowance, but your natural coordination will take care of it. Just look ahead of the target. Look at it as you swing through, then actually look ahead, and that lovely computer between your ears will send your forward hand right where it needs to be. That's the essence of hand-eye coordination. Don't measure the gap between the barrel and the target; you'll slow the swing if you do. And don't try to second-guess the process that's happening naturally. Trust it.

Just flick your eyes to the place where the target's going to be in the next instant, and press the trigger. The next thing you see will be a dead bird or a shattered target.

How far ahead you need to look depends, of course, upon gun speed in relation to target speed and angle. Every shooter has a particular swing-speed that's most comfortable, and you might be surprised at how consistently you maintain that speed from shot to shot. Some practice at targets of varying angle will show what works for you, and the whole process will soon become second nature.

Practice is the key to learning and refining any technique. Chances are this one will seem awkward at first. That's okay. For most of us, learning good habits involves unlearning some bad ones, and it takes a bit of effort. You can get in a lot of good work at home, without firing a shot. Stand in any room with enough space to swing a gun and use the lines where the walls meet the ceiling as references. Imagine they're flight lines. Take up the ready position, imagine that a pheasant has appeared in one corner and is flying toward the other. Pick the spot where you're going to kill him, and practice swinging the muzzles along the line, coming from behind, passing through, looking ahead, and dry-firing with a snap cap. You can change the angle simply by standing at a different place in the room.

You can also use vertical references to practice the moves for rising or dropping targets—wall corners, door frames, trees, powerline poles, any strong vertical line.

At first, concentrate on moving your forward hand first and on getting the swing and mount into one smooth, continuous motion. Then work on tracking the muzzle along the reference lines, using as many different angles as possible. Shoot as many skeet or sporting clays targets as you can. The more you practice, the easier it gets.

Footwork also is an important component. Ignore all the crouches, wide-legged stances, and other contortions you see among trap and skeet shooters. Just stand straight, with your feet five or six inches apart, your left foot (right foot if you're left-handed) slightly forward and pointing to the spot where you're going to kill the bird.

On a target field, when you know where the target's going to be when you shoot, you can set yourself up in advance. In game shooting, you can get set while you're swinging on the bird. I start with my feet together and step toward the bird with my left foot during the swing-and-mount sequence. This is another of Jack Mitchell's little tricks, and it's an excellent way of keeping your balance and flexibility no matter what angle the target takes. Should you decide to adopt this technique, I recommend working on the actual gunhandling first and practice enough to commit the swing and mount to your muscle memory before adding the footwork. It's easier to learn if you go about it in stages.

CARTRIDGES

23

A Case History of the Shotshell

A shotshell case is a wonderfully simple thing, a tube closed off at one end by a thick base with a flanged rim. It's been made of nearly every workable substance known to man—brass, copper, steel, tin, aluminum, zinc, nickel, paper, and plastic. Like most simple things, it's the product of a complex evolution.

If you set aside the various linen and paper pouch-type cartridges that date back at least to the latter sixteenth century, the first recognizably modern shotshell case was the pinfire version that the Frenchman Casimir Lefaucheux designed in the 1830s, followed by an improved version invented by Houllier in 1846. Yet a third Frenchman, M. Pottet, patented in 1855 a cartridge that looks remarkably like a standard shotshell of the early twentieth century. It became the first commercially produced shot cartridge to use a centerfire primer. George Daw, a

London gunmaker, altered Pottet's design of the primer and secured an English patent for the whole cartridge in 1861. Shortly after, the Eley brothers contrived to break Daw's patent, and centerfire shotshells were all the rage in England and on the Continent by 1866.

While European gentry were buying and shooting factory-loaded cartridges by the thousand, American gunners wanted something more durable than the wound-paper cases so popular overseas. Frugal Yankees saw little merit in tossing away a case after only one or two loadings, and the most successful of the early American cases were made of brass. Edward Maynard, a New York City dentist best known for his tape-priming mechanism for military rifles, developed an early shotshell case that comprised a drawn-brass body with a brass head soldered onto it. A standard percussion cap ignited the powder through a tiny hole in the case head. Maynard experimented with self-primed cases through the 1860s and in 1873 came up with a brass-bodied shell with a turned-brass head that could accommodate a Berdan primer.

The Draper shell, patented in 1864 by W.H. Wills and manufactured by F. Draper & Company, also used a standard percussion cap, but unlike Maynard's case, the Draper used a nipple attached to the shell and not the gun. Both the nipple and the case head were separately milled parts that screwed onto a brass body. It must have been horrendously expensive to make.

Actually any brass case was difficult to manufacture before the 1870s, because it wasn't until about 1875 that American technology reached a point where a brass case could readily be formed in one piece. Even then it was no simple matter. The process began with a brass disc. This was formed into a cup and then, through a series of dies and punches, drawn into a finished case 2½ to 3 inches long. The complex shapes of the head and primer pocket were an especially taxing problem, but American ingenuity was such that by 1880 Remington, Winchester, and Union Metallic Cartridge Company all were turning out brass cases by the wagonload. The U.S. government made them, too, at the Frankford Arsenal, first of gilding metal and then, after the mid-1880s, of tinned brass.

A well-made brass case is virtually indestructible. Properly annealed, it will be extremely hard at the mouth, where the metal is thin, and softer but tough in the head. Carefully washed and dried after each use and protected from dents, a brass case can be loaded time after time. They were made in a wide array of gauges—among them 8, 10, 11, 12, 14, 15, 16, 20, and 28—and remained in production for a long time. Remington manufactured brass cases until 1957, and cases made of both brass and zinc were available from Canada well into the 1970s.

Good as the drawn-brass case was, a brass-headed paper case was the classic shotshell for nearly a hundred years. C.D. Leet secured the first American patent for paper cases in the 1860s, followed by Benjamin Hotchkiss, the Englishman Charles Lancaster, and others. Remington, Winchester, and Union Metallic Cartridge all made paper cases along with their brass versions.

Although different manufacturers used slightly different techniques, the typical paper case was made by coating thin paper with glue and winding it onto a mandrel to form a tube with walls about .03-inch thick. The base was also made of wound paper, strips varying in width from about ⅕-inch to nearly ¾-inch; this gave the base a concave inner face, which helped ensure good contact between the priming charge and the powder. Shell bases are still cupped that way.

Once wound, the base was inserted into one end of the paper tube, and a cupped-and-drawn brass head was swaged on to fasten everything together. A narrow hole through the brass formed a flash channel for the primer, and the brass head was crimped into the primer pocket to hold the primer cup in place. With powder, wadding, and shot put in, the case mouth was rolled inward against a thin, hard over-shot card to finish the cartridge.

Never as durable as one made entirely of brass, the paper case still could be reloaded four or five times before heat from the powder burned pinholes through the case wall at the point where the brass head ended. Current paper cases suffer the same fate, and the base and tube eventually part company altogether. Around the turn of the century, manufacturers tried to overcome this and the even more pernicious problem of gas seeping between the base and the tube and blowing out the brass rim. First, they extended the brass head an inch or more up the case body and then began lining paper cases with metal. Winchester brought out the first brass-lined cartridges in 1894. Remington developed a similar design about the same time but in 1912 switched to a steel liner. The liners helped somewhat, but manufacturing expense eventually forced them off the market. As the technology improved, the plain paper case could be made cheaply enough that a few more loadings scarcely mattered.

With one exception, the classic paper case went virtually unchanged for nearly seventy years. In the late 1930s, the over-shot card and roll crimp were discarded in favor of the now-standard star or pie crimp. Popular opinion, which often seeks to justify an economic change by calling it a practical improvement, had it that getting rid of the over-shot card made patterns denser in the center—as if a heavy charge of lead were likely to be disrupted much by an almost weightless wafer of cardboard. Still, the star crimp does have some practical advantages in that it reduces the number of components, simplifies loading, and is easier to seal against moisture.

Good as it was, the old paper hull was doomed by the technology that developed after World War II. The flourishing interest in plastics led ultimately to a wholesale revolution in shotshell design that has made American ammunition the best in the world. Remington Arms brought out the first plastic shell in 1960 and thereby started a trend that has since spread around the world.

Remington called its first plastic case the SP because it had a brass-plated steel head (S) and a polyethylene body (P). Its nonintegral base, made of pulverized paper, was, like that of a paper hull, locked into place by the metal head. It was many things that a paper case could never be—completely waterproof, swell-proof, and astonishingly durable. The slick body fed smoothly through any repeating action.

Winchester also had been experimenting with plastics all through the 1950s, first attempting to form cases by an injection-molding process. None of the available plastics proved suitable. They were too sensitive to temperature, either going so soft in warm weather that the shot column actually dug into the case walls and ripped them apart, or at the other extreme, becoming so brittle with cold that cases split when the cartridges were fired. Winchester finally adapted a German technique called the Reifenhauser process, named after its inventor, and struck upon an economical way to turn granules of polyethylene resin into an extruded tube. Fitted with a base and metal head, it performed superbly as a shell case.

At the same time, Winchester also experimented with ways of forming a complete case, minus only the metal head, from a single lump of plastic. The result first came on the market in 1964. The compression-formed case, as Winchester described it, represented yet another major advance in shotshell design.

By combining aspects of both injection-molding and extrusion processes, Winchester succeeded in producing a one-piece case so resilient that it could readily be fired without the metal head. During the extrusion process, the plastic is worked enough to give the case walls a tensile strength of as much as 35,000 pounds per square inch—which is nearly six times stronger than injection-molded polyethylene. These cases can withstand internal pressures of more than 60,000 pounds per square inch, force enough to blow up any shotgun ever built.

Though polyethylene-tube cases with non-integral bases still are produced, the one-piece plastic case has long been the world standard. All of the important American ammunition-makers crank them out by the millions every year. Other types of plastic cases have come and gone, most of them made of hard, extremely tough material. Some, notably the Wanda and Herter's shells marketed in the late 1960s and early '70s, used friction-fitted plastic over-shot wads rather than pie crimps. A current shell, marketed under the trade name ACTIV, is pie crimped.

ACTIV cases have metal-reinforced rims, but the Wanda and Herter's versions were plastic all the way. Not even the softer plastic cases need them for strength, but metal heads still serve a good purpose. Extractors, especially those in autoloading guns, can chip a plastic rim, leaving the case stuck in the chamber.

Until about sixty years ago, shotshell cases were made proportional to shot charges—which in turn were proportional to bore sizes. The British long ago determined an optimum balance between a gun's weight and the shot charge it fires, that a gun ideally should be ninety-six times heavier than the shot load. Any more weight is unnecessary; any less makes recoil uncomfortable. A gun built for a one-ounce load, then, should weigh six pounds; 1⅛ ounces of shot calls for a 6¾-pound gun; and a 1¼-ounce charge needs a gun of 7½ pounds. English guns are built and proofed for a specific shot charge that in turn implies a standard mean working pressure. That's the main reason why a diet of heavy American cartridges can batter a fine English gun to rubble.

Actually it makes excellent sense to tailor gun and load to one another. It can't be done with mass-produced guns, and that's one of the tradeoffs we make in return for relatively inexpensive, factory-built guns. Tailoring a cartridge case to the shot and powder charges inside makes equally good sense, and that traditionally has been the British approach. The typical English game cartridge, made for the typical English game gun, is 2½ inches long. Heavier shot charges come in longer cases.

This was also true in America until about 1930. Even though there were certain standard case lengths for the various gauges, American shotshells of the early twentieth century came in a multitude of sizes. The variety reached a peak just before

World War I. The 1916 Winchester catalogue lists the following available as factory loads:

Gauge	Case Length (inches)
4	4
8	3, 3¼, 3½, 3¾, 4
10	2⅝, 2¾, 2⅞, 3, 3⅛, 3¼
12	2¼, 2⅝, 2¾, 2⅞, 3, 3⅛, 3¼
14	2 9/16
16	2½, 2 9/16, 2⅝, 2¾, 2⅞, 3
20	2½, 2⅝, 2¾, 2⅞, 3
24	2¼
28	2½, 2⅞
32	2½
.410-bore	2

Most of these, including some standard gauges, were gone forever by the end of the Great War. Given modern economics and the obvious advantages of mass production, it was inevitable that cartridge cases should evolve to a standard length. Because pumps and autoloaders are full of machinery that shuffles cartridges around, the shells have to be of a uniform length or the guns wouldn't work. What variation in case length still remains is minuscule compared with what used to be.

Standard-length cases made of space-age materials have so thoroughly taken over the market that it's hard to find anything else. Except for three-inch 12- and 20-gauge rounds, 10-bore magnums, and .410 skeet loads, virtually everything you can buy comes in a 2¾-inch plastic case. American-made paper shells are still manufactured, but you often have to search for them. A few die-hard traditionalists no doubt are distressed by that—and I must say, no plastic case is nearly so handsome as the old dark-red paper hull with its richly burnished brass head. But what we may have lost in aesthetics we've more than made up in efficiency and reliability. It's hard to imagine that there's much room left for improvement.

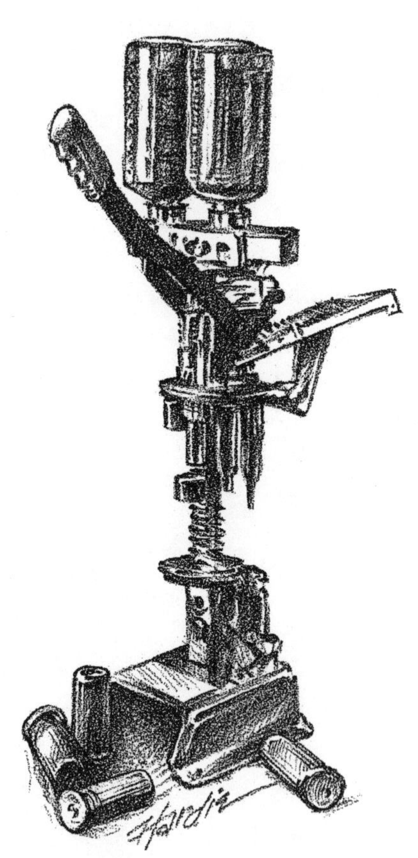

24

When Less is More

For a variety of reasons, we Americans cherish the notion that bigger is better, that more is intrinsically superior to less. Sometimes it is. Apply the idea to woodcock populations, first-class quail habitat, or disposable income, and you'll get no argument from me. Extend the same thinking to cartridges, though, and you'll have to include me out.

Every gauge has its optimum load, worked out by the British a hundred years ago or more, and it functions as the relationship between bore diameter and shot-column length. In short, the optimum load is the maximum quantity of shot a given bore can handle with optimum efficiency, and even though shotgun cartridges are infinitely better than they used to be, optimum loads really haven't changed. The standards still are 1⅛ ounces for 12-gauge, an ounce for the 16, ⅞-ounce in 20-bore, and ¾-ounce for the 28.

The ammunition industry, running full-tilt on the American penchant for making something good into something bigger, has for years seen the standard loads mainly as a point of departure from which to hawk overloaded cartridges with such fanciful, and clearly effective, jargon as "magnum" and "high-power" and "express." If you've ever wondered why the standard American cartridge case is 2¾ inches long while the British still pack their game loads into 2½-inch cases, the answer is simple—our cases are longer because we insist upon putting more shot into them.

Predictably, the ripple effects of this have influenced our view of guns as well. Years ago those who most stoutly championed the 16-gauge often argued that the 16 was "best" because you could "load it up like a 12 or down like a 20." You've heard this litany, no doubt, but tell me: Did you ever know one of these old boys to put a 20-gauge load through his 16?

The same thing happened in turn with the 20-gauge, hailed far and wide for its "versatility"—which of course simply meant that cartridge manufacturers had found a way of stuffing an ungodly amount of shot into it. They did so mainly by resurrecting the three-inch 20-bore case, which had been around since the turn of the century, thereby creating the fabled "20-gauge gun with the 12-gauge load."

In theory and fact the three-inch 20-gauge cartridge is the worst abortion ever foisted upon the gunning world. Here's why. The only way to get more shot into any given bore is to stack the pellets. The longer the shot column in relation to bore diameter, the less efficient the performance, for several reasons. First, the longer column places more pellets in contact with the barrel wall, which scrapes them out of round and turns them into useless flyers. The longer and heavier the shot charge, the more it resists thrust from the powder gases, in part because of increased friction and in part simply because a heavier object is harder to move. This increases chamber pressure and also means more crushed pellets at the bottom of the column;

these string out behind the main swarm, rapidly shedding velocity and contributing nothing to pattern efficiency.

Extra-hard or plated shot protected by a good shot cup and cushioned by a collapsible wad mitigates this to some extent—all the more if the pellets are buffered as well. But even if none of the pellets get battered out of shape, a long shot column in the cartridge still creates a long shot string in the air. This won't show up on your patterning plate, because a stationary plate only shows where the pellets strike in cross-section, not how long it takes them all to get there. What looks like a wonderfully dense pattern more likely is a strung-out mess gaping with holes big enough to throw an Irish setter through.

The bottom line is that the advantages of overloaded rounds are largely illusory. In practical fact, the bloody things aren't worth either the expense or the discomfort. And they are discomfortable in the extreme.

Thanks to Mr. Newton's equal and opposite reaction, the more pressure the powder works up trying to drive a big shot charge out of the case and down the bore, the more force is exerted backwards as well. The greater the pressure, the greater the kick. Recoil makes you fidget and flinch, makes you lift your head away from the gun, makes your whole body tighten up just when it should be loose and flexible, makes you stop your swing, makes you miss.

Here again, I can't think of any better example than the so-called magnum 20. I've fired just about every factory load that's been on the market for the past twenty-five years, and nothing has ever slugged me harder than the three-inch 20 in a lightweight gun.

So what good are 30 percent more pellets if they're giving you less-effective patterns, less-efficient shooting, and beating hell out of you to boot?

The same principle that makes the three-inch 20 such a wretched customer applies to every other gauge as well, although bore size confers some latitude in varying degrees. The smaller the bore, the less tolerant it is of overloads. That's why the typical 28-gauge turns from beauty to beast with anything more than ¾-ounce of shot, and it's also why the .410 is so often unreliable with any load.

Larger bores can much better handle a bit more shot, simply because shot-column height increases proportionately less. That's why a 12-gauge shoots a 1¼-ounce pigeon load so beautifully. Similarly, a 16 will do okay with an extra eighth-ounce of shot—but the 16 behaves so sweetly with a light powder charge behind a one-ounce load that there's nothing at all to be gained from anything heavier.

Even when the shot charge is held to optimum level, too much powder produces its own sort of overload. This probably doesn't wreck patterns quite as badly as too much shot does, but a heavy powder charge doesn't confer any advantage. It's a fact of shotgun ballistics that the faster you drive pellets out of the muzzle, the faster they slow down once in the air. The way to get more punch and more reach is to use heavier pellets, not more powder.

All a heavy powder charge really does is batter you with more recoil, which is not only unnecessary punishment but also a detriment to good shooting.

None of this is to say that there aren't advantages in departing from standard loads, only that the direction we've traditionally chosen has not always been the best one. With few exceptions, adding shot is no improvement. Taking some away, however, can produce astonishing results.

Not so long ago, the notion of reducing the standard shot charge for any gauge was looked upon in this country as the veriest lunacy. After all, if a certain amount of shot is good, then more must be better and less must therefore be worse...or even if less isn't exactly worse, it at least requires compensation by increasing the powder charge.

So the thinking went, and so, to an unfortunate extent, it still goes, kept alive by our infatuation with firepower and the mistaken idea that heavy loads are somehow a fit substitute for good shooting.

Until recently, even optimum loads in game-shooting configurations weren't always easy to find, so badly did the market suffer from epidemic magnumitis. Optimum-load small-bore rounds with any shot larger than No. 9 were particularly tough to come by. Now, however, the American trade is beginning to wise up and offer good cartridges to those who understand that ammunition doesn't have to brutalize a shooter in order to kill a bird. Some new, slow-burning, low-pressure powders have created excellent 12-gauge loads that also are comfortable to shoot. Winchester's 1⅛-ounce Super-Lite target load is extremely good. So is Federal's wonderfully efficient Extra-Lite. ACTIV's Ultra-Lite and Remington's new Duplex target round, which combines Nos. 7½ and 8 shot in the same load, certainly are soft on recoil, but I haven't yet shot enough of them to form an opinion of their performance.

The situation with small-bore ammunition still has a long way to go. Thanks to the growing popularity of sporting clays, some good ⅞-ounce 20-gauge loads of 7½ and 8 shot are available from ACTIV, Federal, and Winchester. Sixteens and 28-gauges continue to be weak sisters in the ammo market, but some useful versions are available in those, too.

I hope these cartridges represent a trend toward lighter loads. If so, there's one further step we can look forward to. It's revolutionary, as American gunning history goes, and it won't catch on overnight, but it'll be the best thing that's happened to ammunition since the plastic hull.

If there are few truly good reasons to shoot anything heavier than the optimum load in any gauge, the converse does not hold true. Reducing optimum shot charges will in most gauges produce extraordinary results. Instead of feeding your favorite bird gun a load better suited to the next gauge larger, try a load traditionally used for the next gauge smaller; you'll be more than pleasantly surprised at what you find.

We have a hundred years of evidence and experience to show that an ounce of shot ahead of a light powder charge performs beautifully in a 12-bore gun. And by "light" charge, I don't mean the typical 3¼-dram, one-ounce field load, which is almost as brutal as a three-inch 20 and, except for International clay-target shooting, nearly as useless. I mean a powder charge of about 2¾-drams-equivalent or three drams at the most, something on the order of a standard English game load.

Here, too, domestic cartridge-makers are beginning to fill the need. One-ounce, 2¾-dram loads are available from ACTIV, Federal, and Winchester. The Winchester offering, loaded in a AA-type case and marketed under the trade-name Xtra-Lite, is especially good. Estate Cartridge Company of Conroe, Texas, manufactures an excellent 1 1/16-ounce 12-gauge load in a 2½-inch case and an equally good 15/16-ounce load in a 2¾-inch case. Word has it that Estate is working on a ⅞-ounce 12-bore load as well.

We've had much less opportunity to try reduced loads in other gauges, mainly because factory cartridges thus loaded simply weren't available here. American makers have yet to produce anything lighter than ounce loads in 16-gauge and ⅞-ounce in 20.

If you're a handloader, there's a whole world of light cartridges waiting to be tried. While the 12-gauge load in the 20-gauge gun is a worthless instrument of torture, a 20-gauge load in a 12-gauge gun is a revelation. So, for that matter, is a 28-gauge load in the same 12-bore.

Current interest in ⅞-ounce 12-gauge loads originated in the late 1970s and early '80s among target shooters seeking relief from recoil and also some relief from the rising cost of shot. At first, those who wrote about these loads almost invariably referred to them as "powder-puff" or "pipsqueak" or some phrase equally revealing of the bigger-is-better attitude that's plagued us for so long.

The cutesy language soon disappeared because everyone who gave them a serious trial reported the same conclusion: 12-gauge rounds loaded with ⅞-ounce of shot may feel like powder-puffs on your shoulder, but they'll smoke targets time after time.

Indeed, they will, and they'll smoke game birds just as handily. My wife and I shoot thousands of them every year at skeet, sporting clays, and game—doves, quail, woodcock, grouse, and feral pigeons. Loaded at 1,200 to 1,220 feet per second with Nos. 8 or 9 shot for targets and copper-plated 7½'s for birds, these cartridges are deadly as lightning. And you can shoot them all day without getting beaten to a pulp. A couple of my favorite recipes are listed at the end of the chapter.

Such wonderful results from 20-gauge loads led me to wonder if an even lighter charge would perform as well, and for the past few weeks I've been testing a recipe that puts a 28-gauge load—¾-ounce of shot—into a 12-gauge cartridge. In a word, the results so far are superb. In my 6½-pound game gun, recoil is practically nil, while striking energy appears to be ferocious. From a cylinder-bore barrel, they consistently shatter clay targets at about forty yards and reduce them to dust at the same distance with a modified choke.

Since most upland birds are killed considerably closer to the gun than forty yards, I have no reason to believe they won't perform every bit as well on doves and quail, woodcock and grouse. Come fall, I intend to find out. This recipe, too, is listed at the end.

As a fringe benefit, both ⅞- and ¾-ounce loads are splendid for beginners, who stand an excellent chance of hitting plenty of targets without any discomfort from recoil.

Reduced loads work for precisely the same reasons that extremely heavy loads don't. Shot columns are quite short relative to bore size. Being lightweight, the charges don't put up excessive resistance to the powder gases, so there's less likelihood of crushed and useless pellets at the bottom of the column, especially with hardened or plated shot.

These factors combine to create short shot strings with relatively few flyers, which in turn creates highly efficient cartridges. They may, in other words, not carry a lot of shot, but the pellets they do carry all reach the target at pretty much the same time. Pellet density is therefore high at almost every point in the shot string's length—and that makes an effective load.

We've been brainwashed for generations to believe that

only a heavy load will kill a game bird, and we've convinced ourselves that the more shot we fling, the more likely we are to hit what we're shooting at. It just ain't so.

No upland bird hunter needs more than an ounce of shot, and you can do just as well with less, because no upland bird needs to be hit by more than five or six well-placed pellets carrying reasonable burdens of kinetic energy. The energy derives from a combination of velocity and mass (pellet size, in other words) and the placement from a combination of accurate shooting and a shot swarm that isn't strung out to hell and gone.

More to the point, you don't have to shoot a bird to dollrags in order to kill it cleanly, and you'll shoot worse, not better, with heavy loads. No amount of shot will do any good if you don't put it where the bird is, and the best shooting in the world cannot compensate for poor ballistics. Either way, less is more.

The following recipes are quoted either from manufacturers' data or were developed and tested by professional ballisticians. Follow them exactly; do not alter quantities or substitute components. As with all reloading information, neither the author nor the publisher have any control over the manner in which these data are used and therefore assume no responsibility.

1. Winchester AA hull, 12-gauge, 2¾-inch
   Winchester 209 primer
   19.0 grains Winchester 452AA powder
   Winchester WAA12SL wad
   ⅞-ounce (382.2 grains) lead shot
   Muzzle velocity: 1,210 fps
   Pressure: 7,100 lup

2. Winchester AA hull, 12-gauge, 2¾-inch
   Winchester 209 primer
   17.8 grains DuPont Hi-Skor 700X powder
   Winchester WAA12SL wad
   ⅞-ounce (382.2 grains) lead shot
   Muzzle velocity: 1,205 fps
   Pressure: 6,700 lup
3. Winchester AA hull, 12-gauge, 2¾-inch
   Winchester 209 primer
   16.0 grains Hercules Red Dot powder
   Winchester WAA12SL wad, with one 20-gauge
   135 card filler in bottom of shot cup
   ¾-ounce (328.1 grains) lead shot
   Muzzle velocity: 1,220 fps
   Pressure: 5,800 lup

Note: This load may not ignite reliably at ambient temperatures below forty degrees Fahrenheit, and probably will not cycle the action of any current autoloading gun.

25

A Hard Look at Shot

After publishing articles on the advantages of light loads, I have received a tremendous flush of mail from shooters who have discovered on their own the advantages of cartridges lethal at only one end of the gun. It pleases me to no end, as any exchange of experience, insight, and opinion always does. I truly believe the only way we'll ever come close to understanding the sweet mysteries of guns and shooting is by sharing what we know and what we think.

Some men pose good, thoughtful questions about the relative merits of hard and soft shot, wondering if pellet hardness has any bearing on a shot swarm's efficiency.

It does, and while a high level of efficiency is desirable in any load, it's especially important for those with light shot charges—because they carry fewer pellets to begin with.

The easiest way to understand why hard shot is more efficient than soft shot is to consider the aerodynamic properties of a sphere, which are, to put it delicately, less than ideal (in plainer terms, "lousy" is no overstatement). Owing to its streamlined shape and pointy nose, a bullet slips through the air without incurring much atmospheric resistance. A round object, on the other hand, contacts the atmosphere with a relatively greater surface area and simply plows along while resistance builds at an enormous rate.

Unlike a round ball fired from a rifle, a shot pellet has no spin to give it stability. On a day with no wind, a perfect sphere, perfectly smooth and of perfectly consistent density around every one of its theoretically infinite number of axes, probably would fly almost perfectly straight—except, of course, for the descending arc imposed by gravity. But every departure from perfection has a negative effect. A rough surface increases drag. Flats, dents, and projections all create uneven resistance, which pushes the object off course. And if our sphere becomes lopsided and therefore heavier on one side than another, it'll tend to change course by itself, following its own area of greater mass.

I'm not a physicist (which is obvious by now if you are one), but it's easy enough to see that a shot pellet is not the ideal projectile. It is, though, the best thing we have for the job we ask of it, and roundness is a key factor in how well it does that job. All well-made shot is reasonably round to begin with; the trick is to make it stay that way after being moved from dead still to 1,200 feet per second in a few milliseconds' time.

If I'm doing the arithmetic correctly, a shot charge accelerates from 0 to about 820 miles per hour in less than the length of your gunbarrel, and the thrust required to accomplish that places the pellets under tremendous stress.

When the powder ignites, shot pellets start moving in a chain reaction rather like the cars in a train. Those nearest the powder start first and literally push into the rest, crushing together until they're all moving. Thus caught between expanding gas and a mass of inert pellets, the shot in the bottom third of the column suffer a terrific momentary compression, sufficient to flatten them to one degree or another. Those at the very bottom take the worst of it, but many others higher up get squeezed hard enough to be dented or otherwise contorted slightly out of round. The hotter the load, the greater the damage.

Once under way, the outer pellets all around the column scrape along the barrel wall, going flat on one side. In the air, these peel off from the main swarm, while the flattened specimens at the tail-end lag behind, spin away, and presently fall spent and useless. Others behave according to the amount of damage they've taken.

These phenomena were most pronounced in the old days, before polyethylene shot-cup wads, but they still apply, and the efficiency of any load still depends to a serious extent upon the number of pellets that get down the bore unscathed.

If maintaining roundness is the goal, obtaining optimum hardness is the best means of success. At the moment, shot covers quite a wide spectrum on that account—from iron pellets that aren't easy to knock out of shape with a hammer, to pure or nearly pure lead shot, which you can almost flatten with a stern look. If iron were as dense as lead, or if lead were as hard as iron, we could simply grab any box of cartridges and be reasonably certain of good results. Since that isn't the case, the uplander's best choice lies somewhere in the middle.

The most common way of hardening lead is by adding antimony, an elemental metal that rhymes with alimony. And a little of either goes a long way. In shot manufactured by the traditional sieve-and-drop method, too much antimony prevents the pellets from rounding up as they fall, but an alloy of about 4 to 7 percent produces wonderfully hard shot pellets—not up to the resilience of iron, but hard enough to stay usefully round when fired down a barrel. How much alloy is enough depends to some extent upon pellet size, since small pellets seem to deform more easily than larger ones.

The trouble with antimony is that it's expensive stuff, and you won't find any in cheap cartridges or in the cheapest bagged shot available for handloading. That's why the various low-end shells offered by all the ammunition companies generally aren't worth a damn as game loads; soft shot produces too many flyers and stringers for efficient patterning and penetration at any range much beyond arm's length. Similarly, cheap bulk shot is okay for informal target shooting, but you won't like it for competitive clays nor for game.

Plating pellets with copper or nickel is another standard approach. But in my experience, simply adding a few microns of some harder metal doesn't make a soft pellet perform any better. A plated pellet that also has a high antimony content, on the other hand, does seem to make a difference, although I'm not convinced that the difference is great enough in general upland shooting to fully justify the extra cost. I shoot a lot of coppered shot at birds, but I also shoot just as much unplated, high-antimony shot, and I can't say that I find one noticeably better than another. In dressing game, I do find quite a few pellets of both types lodged right against the breastbones of grouse and pheasant, still as round as they were in the cartridge, so penetration clearly isn't a problem with hard, unplated shot. The birds certainly never know the difference.

Anyway, all shot that glitters isn't necessarily equal. Plating only becomes truly effective at a certain thickness, and in the cheaper forms, the coating is scarcely deep enough to make the pellets shine. I doubt it contributes anything of practical value. Among factory loads, the copper-plated shot Winchester uses is first-class, and so is the shot in Federal's Premium line. Lyalvale Express offers cartridges loaded with both nickeled and coppered shot; with coatings of ten microns nickel or fifteen microns copper, these ultra-high-performance loads are mainly meant for International target and FITASC competition, but they're also top-notch fodder for long-range upland shooting.

For workaday hunting, unplated high-antimony shot will deliver the goods perfectly well. Ammunition and component manufacturers unfortunately tend to salt their advertising with all sorts of references to hard shot, oblique or otherwise, but the proof doesn't always come out in the pudding. To be certain of getting truly hard shot, the simplest course is to avoid cheap shells and go for top-of-the-line target or pigeon loads. What particular brand you choose doesn't much matter; all ammunition makers of good repute offer excellent target cartridges. They're more expensive than field-type loads, but antimony accounts for most of the extra cost—and if you want hard shot, antimony, not ad copy, is what you're looking for.

Handloaders also can get extra-hard shot, and it, too, is more expensive, but if, as I do, you take a certain pleasure in tailoring the best game loads you can, it's worth the price. Among the more readily available brands, I've had the best results with Lawrence Brand Magnum shot, both plain and coppered. Factory literature quotes the antimony content of Magnum Nos. 7½ and 8 at 6 percent, and considering the performance it's given me, I have no reason to disbelieve it.

If you want to go whole-hog, you can get some Italian-made plated shot that's about as good as shot can get. I have a small bag of Aquila nickeled pellets that I've been nursing along for several seasons, as if it were fine champagne—which it might as well be, comparing prices ounce for ounce. But I get a kick out of loading it into a dozen or so special cartridges every fall for the season's first shots at grouse, my little tribute to the crown prince of upland birds.

Popular wisdom, in some quarters, has it that soft shot is actually an advantage because it produces wider patterns choke for choke than hard shot does. The fallacy here is that the wider spread is a result of all the flyers, and flyers simply are not effective against any but the softest-bodied birds at very close range. On the bigger birds, and on all birds at much distance, flyers are cripplers. If you want wider patterns, have your chokes honed out.

And if you want the most efficient performance from your cartridges, there's no substitute for hard shot.

26

Gunning John Ringneck

Knowing my fondness for lightly loaded cartridges, a lot of readers have written to ask if the same preference extends to pheasants. It does, but with a caution. A lifetime's experience tells me that pheasants aren't exactly like other upland birds.

Along with the bobwhite, John Ringneck was the sweet bird of my youth, although for a while he was harder to come by. In Iowa, when I was a kid, there was no pheasant season in the southern two tiers of counties. This meant the two or three birds that lived on my grandfather's farm would have been fair game just across the road. But unlike the proverbial chicken, they never seemed to cross that road. Instead, they liked to hang out along the railroad that ran through the farm, a quarter-mile south of legal, and test my restraint by flushing right in my face while I was hunting rabbits and quail.

I have to confess, most of my restraint in those days had to do with Granddad's firm promise that I would go gunless for at least the remainder of my life should I even think about shooting one of his pheasants. That kept me on the windy side of the law. Happily, Dad liked hunting pheasants almost as much as he loved hunting quail, so I got my chances to tangle with John Ringneck—not as often as I wished, since the nearest really good pheasant hunting was about a hundred miles from home, but often enough that I fell thoroughly in love with the big gaudy fowl and his go-to-hell attitude.

As the years passed, the birds drifted steadily south, I lived farther north, and as a graduate student at Iowa City in the late 1960s, I finally got to do almost as much pheasant hunting as I wanted. Since then, I've shot them in about seven states, in England, and on the Tisza Plain of southeastern Hungary. What I've learned from it is that getting a pheasant neatly into the game bag can be easy or difficult, depending on the circumstances.

Among upland birds, John Ringneck represents extremes, partly physical and partly what I can only describe as a great determination to go on living no matter what you do to him. He's the largest of gallinaceous birds, apart from turkeys and sage grouse, big-boned and powerfully muscled, and therefore capable of absorbing considerable shock. He is much the same in spirit as in body. For my money, John Ringneck has as much grit as a grizzly bear. Break his wings and he'll run clear out of the county; break his legs and he'll sail twice as far. And either way, if by the grace of chance and a good retrieving dog you should happen to catch him, he'll take you on, too, hand to hand, bare-knuckle and no holds barred. You'll likely win, but you'll know you've been in a scrap.

Which is not to say that pheasants are immune to anything short of artillery. Catch them just right, and you can kill them stone dead with the same load you'd use for woodcock or doves. By "just right" I mean as oncomers, the way you see them on driven shoots. They're the same big, tough birds, but flying high toward the gun, their vitals—head, neck, breast, belly, wings, legs, and all—are exposed. Under those circumstances, an ounce of small shot is plenty, provided you put it where the bird is. I've never shot driven pheasant with anything but a 12-bore gun, but I wouldn't hesitate to use a 28-gauge if I had good ammunition.

Unfortunately, we don't see many oncoming shots in this country, and a pheasant from any other angle can be a different story altogether. The crossing shot is the next most-vulnerable posture, but about 90 percent of missed crossing shots are placed low or behind, or both. A near-miss low might break a wing-knuckle or a leg, and a similar shot behind—made all the more likely by those long, streaming, distracting tailfeathers—might put a few pellets into the body cavity, but in either case, the result is a runner or a sail-off cripple. Shoot low and behind, and you'll just miss.

A pheasant going away is virtually armor-plated: its head is only partially exposed or not at all, hitting a wing is chancy, and almost everything else is shielded by a broad, tough backbone. Trouble is, the way we hunt pheasants, going-away shots are frequent and represent the classic opportunity to rake surprising numbers of feathers off birds that fly on as if nothing happened.

As in all shooting, the problems can lie with ourselves or with the equipment we use. A clean miss is no sin—frustrating at times, but inevitable and nothing to beat yourself up about. On the other hand, birds fringed and feathered, wingtipped, or otherwise merely dinged are a bit sickening. These, too, are not entirely avoidable, but there are some things you can do to keep them to a minimum.

Look first to yourself. Learn a solid shooting technique and stay in practice—and I don't mean firing one box of cartridges on a trap range the weekend before the season opens. If you haven't picked up your gun since last season except to dust it, you can't possibly expect to shoot well come November, and the game fields are not the place to relearn technique and timing every year.

Two things to consider about equipment: No gun or

load, no matter how good, is any substitute for skillful shooting, but the best wingshot alive can't do much if he's inadequately equipped.

What's adequate in this case has relatively little to do with bore size. I've shot almost as many pheasants with 20-gauge guns as I have with 12s, killed a few hundred with 16s besides, and I really can't see any great difference. All three will handle an ounce of shot perfectly well—although the larger the bore, the shorter the shot string tends to be—and an ounce of shot is usually all you need. Sometimes a bit more is helpful; other times you can do just fine with a bit less.

The key, regardless of gauge, is to use the best cartridges you can buy—for all the same reasons you'd want them for other birds, and then some. Hard, well-rounded shot flies straighter, patterns more efficiently, hits harder, and penetrates better, and all the things that make pheasants such magnificent game put a premium on just that sort of performance. Soft, misshapen pellets, flying erratically and shedding velocity, just don't get it done against big, tough birds.

As an impoverished graduate student, I once chose to skimp on ammunition and bought some promotional shells at the local discount house. Like the rest of their kind, they were loaded with cheap, soft shot, and they were loss-leaders any way you looked at them. For the half-dozen I fired, one cockbird came down merely damaged but retrievable, another ran off trailing a broken wing, and two took two solid shots apiece and still flew away streaming feathers. It was the worst day I ever spent afield. On the way home, I stopped on a little backcountry bridge over a tributary of the Iowa River, heaved forty-four brand-new cartridges over the rail, and promised myself I would never again treat a game bird with such shameful disrespect.

Magnum loads are tempting, of course, and I've tried those, too, but you don't need them, not in any gauge. As I've discussed at some length before, exceeding optimal charges of either shot or powder is an exercise in diminishing returns. Anything more than a one-ounce load only sours the 16-bore's sweet nature, and the three-inch 20 is just as worthless for pheasants as it is for everything else.

Magnum thinking has it that increasing the shot charge or the velocity, or both, improves performance, but in a shotgun this is essentially a fallacy. To see why, you need only compare the ballistics of identical pellets fired at radically different velocities.

No. 7½ lead pellets, for instance, behave this way:

Velocity (fps):		
muzzle	20 yards	40 yards
1,330	930	715
1,200	865	675

As you see, the difference of 130 feet per second at the muzzle is reduced by half in the first twenty yards and is down to only forty feet per second at forty yards. Clearly, the faster you start a round object moving through the atmosphere, the faster it slows down. The difference in speed may be substantial at the muzzle, but it's negligible at target distance.

Velocity is only half the equation. The most significant factor is how much energy the pellet imparts to whatever it hits. Compare the same two No. 7½ pellets:

	Energy (ft/lbs):		
	muzzle	20 yards	40 yards
(1,330 fps)	4.91	2.40	1.42
(1,200 fps)	4.00	2.08	1.26

Here, the faster pellet's advantage of almost one full foot-pound of energy at the muzzle is only .16 foot-pound at forty yards. No pheasant would ever know the difference—but the shooter certainly would, because all that initial velocity translates directly into increased recoil. With magnum loads, the only thing that really gets hit harder is the man behind the gun.

While increasing velocity obviously confers no practical advantage, the one thing you can increase to good effect for pheasants is shot size. The larger the pellet, the greater its mass, and the greater the mass, the more energy it carries. For the general round of bird shooting, I like No. 7½ better than anything, and I've killed a lot of pheasants with it—but for all-around pheasant shooting, for being able to deal with the shots as they come, at any angle and reasonable distance, No. 6 is far better.

To see why, compare the energy of a No. 7½ shot with that of a No. 6, both fired at 1,200 feet per second:

	Energy (ft/lbs):		
	muzzle	20 yards	40 yards
No. 7½	4.00	2.08	1.26
No. 6	6.20	3.49	2.23

The No. 6 pellet, which is almost a third heavier than the No. 7½, carries better than half-again the energy out to target distance. Alloyed for hardness, it penetrates muscle and bone extremely well, and if you put a good pattern of it on John Ringneck, he'll go down for the count.

The only problem with No. 6 shot is finding it in factory cartridges of moderate ballistics. A 12-gauge trap load of 6s—1⅛ ounces of shot ahead of a three-dram-equivalent powder charge, for a muzzle velocity of 1,200 feet per second—is excellent for pheasants, but so far as I know, none of the major ammunition companies offers one. No. 7½ is the largest shot available in target-type shells, while No. 6 comes only in the so-called "field" loads that typically contain more powder than anyone really needs. Handloaders can easily get around this, but if you don't roll your own, you're stuck with only a few options. To the ammunition industry, a "light" 1⅛-ounce 12-gauge field load means a 3¼-dram-equivalent charge, for a standard velocity of 1,255 feet per second. The additional speed is utterly useless, but if you choose carefully and buy only top-quality cartridges in order to get extra-hard shot, you can live with it.

Alternatively, you'd do well to consider the standard 12-gauge live-pigeon load, which is 1¼ ounces of shot backed by a 3¼-dram-equivalent charge. Of all the relatively heavy loads available, this is the only one I consider genuinely useful. It's uncommonly well-balanced, for one thing, and at a standard muzzle velocity of 1,220 feet per second, the recoil isn't at all out of proportion to the ballistic results, which in fact can be spectacular—dense, evenly distributed patterns without excessive stringing. Moreover, for reasons no one fully understands, it performs beautifully in almost any 12-gauge barrel.

In the days before steel shot, the pigeon round was my favorite waterfowl cartridge, handloaded with No. 4 shot for ducks and No. 2s for geese, and I killed a lot of pheasants with it as well. You don't always need that much shot, but from experience I have to say I wouldn't object too strongly if someone described a 12-gauge 3¼-dram, 1¼-ounce charge of hard No. 6 as the ultimate all-around pheasant load.

Most of the factory cartridges you'll find in this format will have No. 7½ shot, which is standard for pigeon shooting, but you can get 3¼ - 1¼ loads of No. 6 from at least two of the big three ammunition makers—in Winchester's Super-X Low Brass and in Federal's Premium line, both of which are excellent quality. According to my catalogue, Remington's 3¼ - 1¼ ShurShot load comes only with No. 7½ or 8 shot. If you're a handloader, browse your manuals for 1¼-ounce recipes that develop 1,220 feet per second muzzle velocity. Narrow down even further to the ones that call for the slowest-burning, lowest-pressure powders, and you can make up some pleasant-shooting, wonderfully effective shells.

As I suggested at the start, pheasants pose demands that most other game birds do not, and being properly prepared for them requires special attention.

CONTROVERSIES

Hardie

27

A Heretic's View of Sporting Clays

In 1984 Pin Oak Acres Shooting Grounds, just outside Houston, Texas, was the only sporting clays course in the entire United States. Only a few dozen Americans, who had shot clays in Britain or in Europe, had any first-hand experience with the game. Now, a decade later, courses number in the hundreds, and new ones continue to sprout up like mushrooms on a warm spring night. Shooters number in the tens of thousands.

That sporting clays should catch on so well and grow so quickly is remarkable but not very surprising. Until recently, the target-shooting world idled in doldrums that grew deeper every year. We needed a new shotgun game, one relevant to bird shooting, a game less formalized than trap and skeet, more adaptable than Crazy Quail, and more demanding than targets lobbed, butterflylike, out of a hand-held thrower or a portable trap. The wilting American arms and ammunition industry needed a boost as well.

Sporting clays answers these needs and more. No two courses are alike. Indeed, not even consecutive targets at the same stand are exactly the same, and five minutes' work on the elevation and angle of the trap can change the shot entirely. Using topography and available vegetation, a clever designer can set up shooting fields to present targets that are as birdlike as clay discs can be.

Such infinite variety could hardly help but capture a bird-shooter's fancy, and the game's appeal has in turn made sporting clays the best thing that's happened to our shooting sports industry in a generation or more. More new guns and cartridges have come onto the market in the past three years than in the past twenty—to say nothing of the vitality now humming in the peripheral markets that supply everything from clothing to cartridge bags, earplugs to shooting glasses.

All told, sporting clays has done shooting a world of good—stirred new interest, attracted new people, prompted new technology and new products. It has provided a fine new game to those who enjoy shooting for its own sake. It offers hunters new opportunities to be better stewards of the sport, since good shots waste less game.

This much I believe is true. What other virtues might reside in the bosom of the game depends upon your level of credulousness and your tolerance for blather. Plenty of breathless ink has been dumped on the subject over the past couple of years, and if you care to look, you probably can find someone who's been willing to testify that sporting clays is a sovereign remedy for everything from marital strife to smelly feet.

Maybe so. But the future, as I see it, is not necessarily one of unmitigated bliss. Sporting clays may be the best renaissance that's come to shooting, but it isn't the first, and history holds a lesson worth some thought.

Until sporting clays came along, skeet had more to offer a bird shooter than any other target game. In fact, that whole sport was invented by a grouse hunter as a way of keeping his field-shooting skills in trim. The range layout went public in 1926 in *The National Sportsman* and *Hunting and Fishing*, sister magazines that conducted a contest to give the game a name. Gertrude Hurlbutt of Dayton, Montana, won $100 by suggesting skeet, which is a phonetic spelling of an Old Norse word related to the English *shoot*.

Within two years, skeet fields by the dozen had been built all over the eastern United States, the first national championship had been held, a governing body was organized, and Remington Arms was selling skeet-load cartridges. In the 1930s, when times were tough and game populations dwindled, every sporting magazine in the country promoted skeet as a tonic for ailing gun clubs and conservation-minded hunters. All of the arms-makers brought out guns specially tailored to the game. In 1936, *Hunting and Fishing* estimated the number of skeet fields nationwide at 1,600. Skeet was the fastest-growing, most popular shooting sport in the country.

Fifty years later, it was a moribund exercise in boredom, scorned among bird hunters as artificial frippery utterly irrelevant to field shooting. Some of that sentiment, of course, was largely sour grapes fermented by shooters equally unable to hit a clay target, a game bird, or the backside of a gentleman cow—but there was truth in it nonetheless.

What happened to skeet derived in some measure from its predictability. When the traps are set according to rule-book prescription, targets fly along precisely defined paths. Even though they truly do, in concept at least, represent a great many shots a hunter encounters, the angles are easily memorized. Taking all advantages the rules allow, I daresay that anyone of normal motor skills can, after a bit of coaching and a case of cartridges, turn in a respectable score.

But that's also the rub, because a mania for score was what really turned skeet from dazzling to drab.

The original rules forbade any shooter to shoulder his gun before calling for the target, which makes sense in a game intended to refine field-style shooting. Low-gun skeet is more interesting, more challenging, and far better practice. It's also likely to cost even an extremely good shot a target or two now and then. The best shots of the 1940s and '50s turned in some impressive runs, but widespread agitation in favor of premounting the gun finally won out. Nowadays, skeet is largely an exercise of endurance; the longer you can maintain concentration through shot after tediously repetitive shot, the higher your score, and the game has long since reached the point where runs of five hundred targets or more is minimal qualification for being a serious contender. The burnout rate among good shots is quite high.

Although skeet always has been a far more relaxed and friendly game than trap, all the emphasis on cumulative scores, averages, classifications, and the other rubbish that goes with competition puts off a lot of people who might like to shoot simply for fun. Beginners can easily be intimidated by what appears to be great skill on the part of even middling shooters and shy away before they have a chance to learn how easy skeet really is.

Under the circumstances, it's small wonder that sporting clays has been met with such enthusiasm, not only among target shooters but among hunters as well. So far, the game remains true to its historical purpose, which is to duplicate as closely as possible the conditions and challenges of field shooting.

But history is cyclical, and some of the same things that ultimately took much of the fun out of skeet are beginning to loom over sporting clays. Big-money tournaments sprang up early on, and with them came systems of classification, registration, and the rest. Two separate sanctioning bodies are wrangling with one another, maneuvering for control over registered competition and the power to establish rules of the game.

In short, preoccupation with score already has exerted considerable influence over sporting clays. Those who enter high-stakes matches are beginning to insist that means be devised whereby every shooter should have precisely the same shot at a given stand—an understandably democratic view but a difficult thing to accomplish in a game whose interest depends to a great extent upon variability. There's even talk of allowing premounted guns.

Arguably, none of this affects those who don't care to compete, who simply want to shoot for fun and for practice when the bird seasons are closed. Perhaps. But I'm not convinced. I have no quarrel with anyone who likes competition—until it begins to interfere with those who don't. And I see a certain attitude accruing to sporting clays that disturbs me: a subtle implication that score is the be-all and end-all of reasons for shooting; a suggestion that if you can't score well, you have no business being on the course; an inclination to follow every missed target with a surge of gastric acid and words of Anglo-Saxon etymology.

Sporting clays' popularity predictably has spawned a spate of "expert instructors." Some of them really are. Others are charlatans, bozos, and assorted clods who attempt to make the simple, elegant act of shooting into something complicated and arcane, mainly to impress you with how much *they* know that *you* don't. Their attitude seems to be that if you don't do it their way, or with a gun like theirs, you're doing it wrong.

It's all fairly subtle, but it has a cumulative effect. I've met lots of people who've said they're intrigued by the idea of sporting clays—but they've read so much about how difficult it is, and how good a shot you have to be, and how you have to have the "right" gun...on and on. The fact is, they're intimidated by the whole game and don't want to embarrass themselves. No one does. The sad part is that there's nothing inherently embarrassing or intimidating about sporting clays; the problem lies in the atmosphere growing around it.

If you know the feelings I'm talking about, let's speak plainly:

You don't need the "right" gun for sporting clays. It was meant to be shot with field guns. Nor do you need screw chokes or battery-driven choke wrenches. You may one day decide to buy a specialized clays gun—there are some extremely good ones on the market—but believe me, you can have just as much fun with your favorite fowling piece, whatever it is.

If keeping score bothers you, don't. You don't have to. Tell the range officer or trapper you're not interested in keeping score, and if he makes you feel in any way uncomfortable about it, go elsewhere to shoot. After all, you're paying the fee.

If any shooting stands or fields don't appeal to you for some reason, don't shoot them. You don't have to attempt every shot on the course just because it's there, and besides, any shot that isn't reasonably birdlike is a poorly designed presentation anyway.

Shoot with like-minded people. You'll meet some nice chaps at every course and they usually outnumber the yo-yos. If you only want to shoot for fun, go with those who feel the same way.

Don't be intimidated by what you've heard or read about the game. Some shots are tough, and some aren't, but nobody hits them all.

Above all, relax and have a good time. The point isn't how many targets you break or miss. As I see it, any day spent shooting is a good one, even those not-infrequent days when I'm hard-pressed to hit the ground with my hat. The point is to enjoy the experience, and sporting clays offers the best opportunity in years to do just that. If we're careful not to take the game, or ourselves, too seriously, it can stay that way for a long time to come.

28

Women and Shooting

The five women knew full well what a stir they were about to cause, but if they felt self-conscious, they showed only good humor and good grace. They had come to the Everett Gun Club at West Everett, Massachusetts, simply to shoot—the only competitors in the first official women's skeet shooting tournament. If you'd asked them what they thought about a tournament open only to women, all five probably would have said the same thing: It's about time. It was Wednesday, June 19, 1932.

Four lived in Massachusetts: Anna Mary Vance, Gertrude Wheeler, Gertrude Travis, and Mrs. Walsworth Pierce. Peggy Small had come all the way from Detroit. All five wore cloche hats, and skirts that reached below the knee. Only Gertrude Travis was unmarried at the time.

The event was fifty targets. Mrs. Pierce, shooting a 16-gauge autoloader, and Gertrude Travis, shooting a 20-gauge double, each broke thirty-four. Anna Vance and Gertrude Wheeler both shot autoloaders, Mrs. Vance a 16-bore and Mrs. Wheeler a 12. They broke forty-three targets apiece. Peggy Small won the tournament with a 20-gauge double and a perfect score of fifty straight.

In a mixed-pairs shoot that followed, Mrs. Small broke another twenty-five straight, dropped two targets in the fourth round and finished with ninety-eight of a hundred. Then she borrowed a .410 and broke nineteen, just for the fun of it.

Shooting clearly was fun for Peggy Small. At the time, she held the women's long-run record at skeet with eighty-one consecutive hits. In April 1934, she extended it to 131 straight, still using her 20-bore double. Skeet was still in its infancy then and was a substantially more difficult game than it is today.

The writer who covered the 1932 tournament for *National Sportsman* made the predictable allusions to the goddess Diana and concluded his report by observing that "there is no reason why ladies cannot enjoy Skeet and shoot it as well as men." It's a proper sentiment, but I'm not sure he really believed it, for much of his article has a tone of slightly breathless wonder, as if he wasn't completely convinced that what he witnessed had actually happened.

Similar sentiments unfortunately are still with us. In the mildest form, it is simply a patronizing attitude toward women who shoot, as if a woman with a gun were an amusing anomaly not to be taken seriously. The radical view seems to have it that any woman who shoots, particularly if she shoots quite well, is a predator of menacing intent and ambiguous plumbing. Both opinions are utter nonsense, but they do exist.

There are plenty of sociological reasons why relatively few women take up shooting but not one valid reason in Creation why any woman cannot shoot splendidly if she chooses to do so.

American women have done just that for a hundred years. Annie Oakley's exhibition and trick shooting earned worldwide fame in the 1880s and '90s, but she also was a superb live-pigeon and clay-target shot. Women truly came into their own as target shooters in the 1930s. Marie Kautzky Grant—daughter of Joseph Kautzky, inventor of the Fox-Kautzky single trigger—was Iowa's state trapshooting champion eighteen times between 1923 and 1947. Lela Hall, an equally brilliant trap shot, won the Missouri state championship time and again. Between them, Mrs. Grant and Mrs. Hall owned virtually every national championship in women's events and a healthy number in open events as well.

Peggy Small and Anna Vance dominated women's skeet shooting through the mid-1930s, succeeded by Patricia Laursen and Jean Smythe, who held world records in 1941 and '42. Since World War II, skeet has produced a host of fine shots: Ann Martin; Carola Mandel, who in 1954 was the 20-gauge world champion of all skeet shooters; Kathleen Dinning; Ann Yancy; Karla Roberts; and Lori Desatoff, who has held virtually every women's high-average title since 1982.

I have taught several women to shoot, both formally and informally, and I believe I've learned more from them about the nature of shooting than they ever learned from me. From that experience, I'd argue that if a man and a woman, both beginners, were given good instruction and equal practice, the woman most likely would become the better shot in a shorter time.

Attitude is the key. I have yet to meet a woman who believes that being born female implies an innate ability to handle a gun. The converse is not true for many men. Because women tend to look on shooting as simply an acquired skill, which it is, they can approach it unfettered by some unnecessary pressures. An ability to shoot isn't part of anyone's sexual identity, male or female, but many men, especially young ones, seem to have a hard time learning that. Some never do.

None of the women I've taught were defensive about being a novice, and that gave them an important advantage: they could concentrate on learning to hit a target without fretting over what it meant to their egos if they missed. Hand-eye coordination, the physical crux of shooting, works best when the conscious mind is undistracted—and stuffing pieces of your ego into a gun along with the shells is a major-league distraction.

Despite the cherished notions of the macho set, women are no more inherently recoil-shy than men nor any more susceptible to its cumulative effect. Given a well-fitted stock of proper length and pitch, with a good bit of cast at the toe, a woman in good physical condition can absorb as much recoil as anyone. Those who shoot hundreds of cartridges at trap tournaments certainly do, and a registered trap shoot these days can be as much an endurance contest as a game of skill.

I once overheard one knuckle-dragger chortling to another over how he had "cured" his wife's interest in learning to shoot by giving her his duck gun and a handful of three-inch shells. I trust there is a particularly hot corner in Hell reserved for such types. That might help cure what really needs curing.

There are men who pine and sigh because they have no sons with whom to share their fondness for shooting. But all too many of them never seem to think of asking their daughters if they'd care to give it a try. Perhaps they see shooting simply as an adjunct to hunting and assume their daughters wouldn't enjoy hunting. Maybe they wouldn't, but hunting is a separate matter and there is no reason at all why anyone cannot enjoy target-shooting for its own sake.

Clearly somebody has been encouraging daughters to shoot. In 1930, the National Skeet Shooter's Association, forerunner of the current NSSA, estimated that there were about a hundred female skeet shooters in the United States—a minuscule fraction of the total number of skeeters. At the end of 1985, women made up slightly less than 7 percent of the memberships of both NSSA and the Amateur Trapshooting Association. The numbers are lower than they ought to be, but the trend is encouraging.

One of the pleasantest memories I have from competitive shooting days is of coaching a women's collegiate trapshooting team, five young women who hadn't three hundred targets-worth of experience among them when we started.

They accepted me readily enough and took seriously the business of learning to shoot. By the end of the season they'd outshot every team they'd gone against. Just for fun, they took on the campus men's team, which I also coached, and outshot them, too. It had little to do with my teaching ability. They broke every target all by themselves and never got angry or glum over a miss. They were simply five good shots who took keen delight in playing the game. They won the championship trophy that year and gave it to me. I still have it.

29

Flying Your Guns

Thanks to the flying machine, the world is a profoundly smaller place than it was two generations ago—which, among other things, has created opportunities for sport that our grandparents scarcely dreamed of. You and I can leave home any morning of the year and find ourselves hunting game in some far-off place less than a day later. That I get to do this sort of thing fairly often is one of the more pleasant aspects of my job, but it never fails to boggle my imagination. Sometimes, high-speed air travel simply seems too good to be true. And sometimes it is. Instead of enjoying the hunting trip to which you've invested time and money, you can find yourself sitting in some airport wondering what happened to your gun. You can come up with a makeshift substitute for almost any other piece of equipment, but a lost or damaged firearm spells the difference between a dream trip and a nightmare.

Depending upon where you're going and what you're hunting and the outfitter you're working with, taking your own gun isn't always necessary. I've used borrowed guns on a couple of trips, however, and even though it worked out well enough, I've since decided not to do that again except under unusual circumstances. Using my own guns is a large part of the pleasure I get from hunting—large enough to be well worth the risk.

Actually, the risk needn't be great. We all know someone who can tell sad tales about traveling with guns. Any trip can go wrong because of faulty planning or an unexpected quirk of fate, but the fact is, you can do quite a lot to ensure that your guns arrive safe and sound.

First, determine whether the airline you plan to use accepts firearms. So far as I know, all of the major companies do, but some smaller ones don't, so it's wise to check out every carrier you'll be using on the trip. There's no fun in getting to the last leg and learning that Aldertop Air will take you but not your gun.

A word of caution here for riflemen: Terry Wieland tells me that some bush-plane-type airlines that do carry firearms won't accept full-length hard cases, simply because they won't fit into the baggage compartments of very small planes. Be sure to ask about that and be prepared with a soft case or scabbard for the trip into the bush.

While you're checking, ask about the degree of liability each carrier accepts for baggage. For most, the limits are less than the cost of replacing even a moderately priced gun, and you need to know up front what the airline is willing to do in the event of loss or damage. Also ask if you can buy additional insurance for your gun. Most airlines offer that service, but some don't. Your travel agent should be able to get answers to all these questions when he books your flights.

If you insure your gun through an airline, be aware that the coverage is good only for the time you're actually traveling—that is, during the time when the company has possession of the gun as part of your baggage—although one policy purchased with a round-trip ticket covers your gun both ways.

Even if additional insurance is available, the upper limit may not be enough to fully cover an expensive gun. Check that out, too. If you travel to hunt more than once or twice a year, you're probably better off insuring your guns privately and individually. For a relatively small annual premium, you can insure against any sort of loss or damage anywhere you take them. I've done this with the guns I most often use and travel with, and it promotes a satisfying peace of mind.

The Federal Aviation Administration has established certain basic regulations on transporting firearms. These are simple and straightforward. The key points are that firearms must be unloaded; must be declared to the airline; must be checked as baggage; and must be in airline-approved containers. Other regulations and restrictions are the prerogative of individual airlines.

The most important item here, at least in terms of passenger prerogative, is the choice of container. A hard case with some sort of lock on it generally will satisfy airline requirements, but not every hard case is equally good. If you do much flying at all, you have only to look at your suitcases to realize that baggage takes a beating. Airlines really don't employ a special staff whose job it is to bash luggage, but it sometimes seems that way.

What you need is a case that offers optimum protection and security. On the protection side, look for one made of highly durable material, with a piano-hinge lid that forms at least a partially waterproof seal. It should be fully lined with some sort of closed-cell padding. Open-cell material, like common foam rubber, is too easily compressed to absorb shock and still protect a gun.

Molded-plastic cases are okay but not, to my mind, ideal. I've traveled a fair amount with an Italian-made case that has held up reasonably well, but I don't entirely trust it. Temperature seems to affect all plastic to one degree or another, and most become brittle when they're cold—which a gun case is likely to be in an unheated baggage compartment at high altitude during the cooler months of the year. In my experience, and that of quite a few people I know, plastic cases are fine for car trunks and pickup trucks but decidedly risky in the hands of an airline.

A stout, well-built metal case is a far better choice, and there are several on the market. Orvis has one that appears to be extremely good; it's got all the right features and seems plenty sturdy, but I have no firsthand traveling experience with it. I have, however, gone about a jillion miles with one of the superb little trunks built by Americase, and I must say I've never had a case that pleased me more. It's been slung around by baggage handlers on three continents, and even though it shows a few scuffs and scrapes, the latches and hinge still work perfectly, the lid fits as tightly as the day I got it, and there isn't a serious dent to be found—this despite the fact that I once watched through a plane window as it fell off the top of a stack of luggage in a pickup bed and landed on a concrete runway. Through it all, none of the guns inside have suffered so much as a scratch. I don't know what more you could ask.

The toughest case in the world can't offer complete protection if anything inside can be jarred loose. A cleaning rod, snap cap, oil bottle, or anything else rattling around can perform an incredibly destructive dance on a gun, so make doubly sure that everything is secure and block up any free space inside the case with additional padding. A sheet of foam laid over the gun works well; so does bubble-wrap packing material. Whatever you use, make sure it's thick enough to compress a bit between the gun and the lid when you close the case.

Finally, be sure your name and address are on the case, inside and out. An engraved nameplate riveted onto the outside is far better than a removable tag, and a business card slipped underneath the padding inside can be a bit of extra insurance.

If protecting your gun against damage is vital to a successful trip, so is protecting it against the attentions of sticky-fingered types, some of whom are deucedly clever. Last year a good friend of mine arrived home from a shooting trip in Europe and found an empty case waiting at the baggage claim, minus the matched pair of game guns he'd packed into it the day before. The culprits apparently picked the combination locks and relocked the empty case before sending it on. The FBI recovered the guns, but not all such stories have happy endings.

Theft of airline baggage is a federal offense, and federal authorities take such things seriously. So do airlines, since every certified passenger line must, to quote FAA regulations, "ensure that cargo and checked baggage carried aboard the airplane is handled in a manner that prohibits unauthorized access." Because they are responsible both to their customers and to the FAA, airlines generally are quite responsive in dealing with theft.

None of which is much comfort when you arrive in Bumfiddle, Montana, without your gun. A stolen gun, I should point out, isn't the same thing as delayed or misrouted luggage. If your gun isn't on the same plane you are, immediately check with airport personnel to see if it's been delayed. That's happened to me a couple of times; it's inconvenient, but "better late than never" is a good motto to keep in mind when traveling with a gun. The important thing is that it be secure and undamaged when it does show up.

As with protection, there are several things you can do to heighten security. For one thing, choose a case on which every latch is also a lock. I haven't yet seen a case lock that couldn't be sprung or jimmied, given enough time, but the more locks it has, the less attractive it is to someone looking for a quick heist. (Locking latches have another advantage in that they can't be accidentally sprung and damaged by other luggage, baggage-handling machinery, or the like. If your case has any nonlocking latches, keep a roll of duct tape in your carry-on bag and tape them firmly after you declare the gun.)

My pal Bryan Bilinski came up with a great idea for extra security: a plastic-coated, hardened-steel bicycle cable, wrapped around the gun case, through the handle, and fastened with a stout padlock. Nobody who has only a few minutes to attempt a theft will tackle that.

Perhaps the best security of all is a gun case that doesn't look like a gun case. Unfortunately, not many good cases look like anything else, but you still have some options. You must declare your gun to the airline when you check it in, and domestic airlines require you to sign a tag certifying it to be unloaded, but once you've done that, nothing in federal regulation says you can't then put the whole case into some larger piece of luggage—a duffel bag or something similar.

Actually, no regulation says you can't take your gun apart and carry the pieces in more than one bag, so long as you declare it beforehand. Opening all your bags to show the gun at the ticket counter could be inconvenient, but it's an option. The important thing to remember here is that you may not carry ammunition in the same piece of luggage as the gun, nor can you legally transport a gun, ammunition, a hunting knife, or any sort of weapon in a carry-on bag. All such things must go into your checked baggage. Do not try to circumvent these rules; you won't get away with it, and you'll find yourself in a world of trouble, to boot.

For reasons that make no sense at all to me, the standard firearms tag is a piece of blaze-orange cardboard instantly visible at any distance under half a mile. You might as well plaster the case with a sign that says, "If you're looking for something to swipe, try this one!"

But here again you have an option. Even though you must sign the tag and attach it to your gun case, nothing in the federal regulations requires it to be left hanging out for all the world to see. So far as the FAA is concerned, you can sign the tag, stick it inside the case, lock it up, and ship it on. According to Garth Wake, an FAA security manager who was very helpful in providing information for this chapter, each airline can set up its own rules on tags. Some airlines have told me they prefer the tag outside the case, but not all have objected when I insisted upon putting it inside.

As I said earlier, luggage sometimes gets delayed. It's one of the standard inconveniences of air travel, but you can take some preventive measures. Ask your travel agent to book your trip with at least a one-hour layover each time you change planes and at least two hours if you change airlines. Even a moderately busy airport handles an enormous number of bags every day, and the more time you allow the baggage handlers, the better able they are to get your luggage to the right place at the right time. This is a good policy for any trip, doubly so if you're taking a gun.

When you arrive at the airport to begin the journey, bypass the curbside check-in, if there is one, and take your bags and gun to a ticket counter. Most curbside check-ins can't take firearms anyway, but in any event, I always feel more comfortable handing my guns over to a ticket agent.

If your flight bookings are such that you have to claim your bags and recheck them at some point, once again take them to a ticket counter.

Never, under any circumstances, attempt to carry a firearm into a boarding area. *Sporting Classics* editor Chuck Wechsler tells a truly hair-raising story about trying to recheck his rifle while changing flights in Denver, being invited by an airport employee to pass through a boarding-area security point, and instantly finding himself in the company of two FBI agents who detained him for several hours while the whole thing got sorted out.

Do not expect federal security people to dismiss even an innocent mistake out of hand. It's their job to treat any violation of security as a serious matter. If you're uncertain about what to do with your gun, ask to see a security supervisor or an airline representative. But don't take it anywhere near a boarding area.

Despite the potential complications, traveling with a gun is a relatively simple matter, particularly if you have some idea of what to expect and plan your trip accordingly. Copies of appropriate federal regulations are available from any U.S. Government printing office, and the airlines can provide information on their particular policies. Don't be put off by horror stories; learn from them. The air-travel industry is not unlike the postal service in that we hear more about its failures than its successes, even though successes are many times more frequent. Literally thousands of hunters and shooters travel by plane every year without a hitch, and given some good preparation, there's no reason why some of those successful trips shouldn't be yours.

30

Nifty Tricks

The more I think about it, the more certain I am that the most fundamental genre of sporting literature is neither the book, the magazine article, nor the essay. I think it's the tip, the nifty trick that helps advance our way of life yet one more step from primal chaos.

The tip is the tribal lore of sport, passed down from generation to generation. It's our basic unit of cumulative knowledge, our atomic particle, our building-brick in the edifice of communal wisdom. In codified form—as in *The Boy Scout Handbook* or "Tap's Tips"—it is dogma, the outdoorsman's holy writ, but it's equally amenable to humbler uses, losing none of its dignity when asked to serve no purpose loftier than filling space at the tail end of a magazine column.

There's no end to what you can learn from tips, and as a kid, I was a hopeless junkie for such nuggets of information.

Trivial or profound, pedestrian or exotic, it was all the same to me, although I was especially fond of tips that hinted of high adventure: "Three Ways to Get Your Foot Out of a Bear Trap" or "How to Find True North Using a Dead Elk," that sort of thing. At the time, I couldn't see much likelihood of ever actually practicing such arcane skills, but I thought it wise to be prepared, just in case. You never know.

As it turned out, I was right. Through vast good fortune, I've lived long enough and spent enough time hunting and shooting and poking around odd corners of the world that I've been able to put at least some of these gems of woodcraft to the test.

The results have been uneven. I'm happy to report that the standard techniques for disengaging a fishhook from human flesh work pretty much as they're supposed to.

On the other hand, dog lore, which occupies an enormous subset of popular wisdom, strikes much closer to home. Any bird hunter is likely to be a dog man as well, and you should know, if you don't already, that some of our fondest tips on matters canine are real bummers. I've read all the ways of getting porcupine quills out of a dog and tried enough of them to know that the best thing you can do for your quill-stuck pooch is take him to the nearest vet. It'll be a far less traumatic experience for everybody.

Along the same lines, those who most devoutly preach the doctrine that tomato juice will neutralize skunk scent are, I suspect, those who haven't tried it. Years ago a friend's Labrador did some break-dancing on a dead skunk while she was supposed to be hunting grouse. Since the difference in sheer stink between a dead skunk and a live one is about the same as between a live one and Chanel No. 5, the situation called for heroic measures. It was either that or shoot poor Wendy and use her carcass as buzzard repellant.

We bought every ounce of tomato juice on the shelves of the local Red Owl and filled the bathtub in our motel room to the point where she was literally swimming in the stuff. As I recall, we even added some V-8 just to be

sure. We might as well have dumped in a few quarts of vodka and climbed in ourselves. Umpteen gallons of juice and two bottles of shampoo later, she could still bring tears to your eyes from a hundred yards downwind. She slept in the truck during the rest of the trip, and for weeks afterward you never had to wonder where Wendy was.

I've since discovered that nothing deskunks a dog quite so well as a thorough soaking with white vinegar and water mixed in equal proportions.

Even tips that don't work out have a certain charm about them, but those that do are sources of endless delight. They are to me, anyway. I love learning nifty new tricks for accomplishing this or that. The thornier the problem, the better. I like simple solutions that work, and best of all I like the things I learn directly from other shooters and hunters. These truly represent the tribal wisdom of the brotherhood, shared means of solving problems that affect us all.

One of my all-time favorites is a humane, quick, and apparently painless way of dispatching a wounded bird. Neck-wringing, even though it works, never has pleased me much, and I'm even less fond of bashing heads against a tree or a gunstock. I'm not squeamish about it; it just strikes me as disrespectful to treat a game bird so brutally.

Curt Mottesheard, my quail-shooting partner, showed me a better way. With the bird in hand, grasp it by the back with your thumb and forefinger on either side of the spine between the ribs and the legs. Pinch in hard under the spine, and hold the pressure; in just a few seconds, the bird will flutter slightly and then quietly expire. Give it a few more seconds to be certain, and you have a humanely killed, unruffled bird.

I don't know exactly why it works, but I suspect the pressure paralyzes either the heart or the lungs, perhaps both. At any rate, it's gratifyingly quick and gentle, and it works on every sort of bird.

In return for that little jewel, I showed Curt the bird-dressing technique I learned from the employees of a quail-shooting plantation in Mississippi. I imagine every Southerner knows it already, but for my fellow Yankees, it goes this way. Skin the birds and clip off wings, head, and lower legs with poultry shears (which are, by the way, the greatest bird-cleaning tool ever invented). Then snip all the way along one side of the spine from tail to wishbone; do the same thing on the other side, take hold of the neck, pull the spine free, and most of the entrails will come out with it. Even if they don't, it's much easier to take out bits of lung tissue and other offal with the bird laid fully open along the back than it is to dig blindly inside a body cavity. You can get all the tripes and innards out, and there's less risk of infection from gouging your fingers on splintered bones.

This works well on birds of all sizes, though it's an especially handy way to deal with the smaller ones.

Field dressing generally is a big-game hunter's task, but it can be useful to bird shooters as well. After a long day in the fields or the woods, cleaning game comes in dead last on my priority list, well below getting my dog fed, dried off and bedded, finding a stiff snort of whiskey, wiping down my gun, having a hot shower and a good dinner. Depending on where I am, the birds either get strung up in the basement, tucked into a refrigerator, or simply left in the back of the Blazer if it's a chilly night.

They'll keep perfectly well that way for a surprisingly long time. The British, in fact, customarily hang their pheasants for as long as two weeks, and I've never eaten pheasant in England that wasn't delicious. Even if you store them no longer than overnight, however, it's not a bad idea to draw the entrails and let the body cavity cool. As my old friend Ted Lundrigan showed me years ago, you can do that in the field with no trouble at all.

To make the slickest job of it, you need a bird knife, which is simply a pocketknife with a slender blade at one end and a folding hook at the other. Mine is a Buck, but you can get good ones from several knife makers.

Start by plucking enough feathers from around the bird's vent so that you can see what you're doing. Then open the body cavity with a lateral cut just above the vent, switch from the blade to the hook and pull the entrails out. (It's a rare bird that isn't hosting some sort of internal parasites, so if your dog has the same taste for bird guts that mine does, you might want to hang the offal out of reach on a bush or under a rock.)

When the major innards are out, cut the vent and lower gut free, stuff a handful of grass into the body cavity, and you're done. It's a tidy, two-minute job that saves both work and worry at the end of the day. (You may, however, have to explain things to any nonhunters who might be around. After examining my birds without comment for quite some time, my daughter, about eight years old then, finally asked, "Paz, how come all the birds you shoot have grass sticking out of their butt?")

Now that twist-off bottlecaps are more or less ubiquitous in this country, the bottle-opener—or beer wrench, as we called it in the long-gone days of youth—is an all-but-forgotten tool. Forgotten, at least, until you find an old-style cap standing firmly between a roaring thirst and whatever's available to slake it. It's easy enough to pop off a cap on a car bumper, a fencepost, or even a rock if you can find one with the right sort of edge, but if you're hunting or shooting, you have an excellent bottle-opener right in your pocket.

I learned this trick in Mexico, where shooting is thirsty work and where there's no such thing as a twist-off cap on bottles of soda, fruit juice, mineral water, or cerveza. Bottle-openers seem to be an equally rare commodity, but the guides and bird boys simply use a cartridge rim. My weakness for nifty tricks being what it is, I naturally had to try it myself. It took only a couple of miscues, one soaked glove, and a wet pantleg before I got the hang of it, so you should be able to do it first try.

The trick is to squeeze hard on the bottle neck—which gives you a firm fulcrum and also saves you from a bruised hand—and to make sure the pressure you apply against the cap goes upward rather than outward. Empty hulls or loaded shells work equally well.

Finally, a nifty trick with no practical application at all, but one that's great for impressing your friends, especially rifle types who can reel off bullet weights and trajectory tables by the yard.

Every gunner knows the relative relationships among shot pellets—that a No. 4 shot is bigger than a No. 6, and so on. But how many know exactly how big any pellet is? Easy; just subtract the nominal pellet size from 17, and the number you get is the pellet diameter expressed in decimal fractions of an inch. Subtract 2 from 17, for instance, and you know that No. 2 shot measures .15-inch in diameter. No. 6 measures .11-inch, No. 7½ .095-inch, and so it goes.

Unfortunately, no one has come up with a similarly simple formula for figuring the proper lead on a woodcock that seems to be flying in three directions at once, nor a way to erase every yip and flinch from a round of sporting clays, nor a way to remove wad-fouling from a gunbarrel just by squinting hard down the bore. Actually, I'd settle for something that'd proof my dog against cockleburs and cowflops—nothing elaborate, necessarily. Just a tip would do.

31

Epilogue: Knowing How, Knowing When

He always smelled like sunburn and prairie wind, and I thought he was the greatest wingshot who ever lived. He wore high-topped leather boots cross-laced, a tattered, blood-stiffened canvas coat, and carried a Remington pump gun with an action slick as buttered silk.

He had a ribby, soft-eared pointer who rode on the car seat next to him and who could eat up mile after mile of cornfield and foxtail edge at an easy lope. The Texas Ranger loomed in her blood a few generations removed, and the Stud Book knew her as Accolade's Wig Wag. He called her Cookie.

The two of them knew quail in those days—birds twenty or thirty to a covey and in coveys numerous enough that even a middling shot could become a good one without going near a target range.

He was a splendid shot, a natural—unhurried and cool while those little brown bodies came rocketing up around him, tender in the way he smoothed down the ruffled feathers of those that Cookie brought back. When he missed, he'd grin after the departing bird as if sharing a private joke with an old friend.

He never taught me to shoot, not in any systematic way. He simply suggested that I'd do better if the gunbarrel were ahead of the bird and still moving when I slapped the trigger. That worked well enough, but not so well that I could get to be as good as he was. Looking back, I have a notion that he really didn't know how he did it, that explaining how he could hit a fast-moving object with a charge of shot was as baffling as describing the mechanics of how he could hit a golf ball or a fastball, sink a breakaway hook shot, or perform any of a half-dozen such acts in aid of which nature had provided exceptional vision and a level of hand-eye coordination that most of us lack.

So, he didn't exactly teach me to shoot, but he taught me something better.

I was of that bloodthirsty, not particularly attractive age when we're infatuated with our abilities, thin and puerile and untempered as they are. It was late in the afternoon, half-past four perhaps, and gathering sundown. We'd spent the day hunting quail, found and flushed a last covey not a quarter-mile from the car. He took one, and so did I, a tough shot that felt right when it came together, demanding enough that he gave me an extra compliment as Cookie brought it in.

We walked on a little way and sat down to see, as he always said, what there was to see. Whatever it was, I didn't see it. Instead, I played that last shot over in my mind like a foot of film spliced into a loop. Presently, a quail whistled not far off, voicing the sweet, two-tone interrogative that quail use to find their coveymates.

I homed in on the sound and started to get up. He stopped me.

"You already know how to use your gun," he said. "It's more important to know when." And, having heard what he waited to hear, he stood and walked off toward the car.

Twenty-five years later, he gave me the other half.

He was an old man then, grown thin and bent and cloudy-eyed. It was his birthday, and I came back to take him hunting. Cookie was a long-ago memory gone to dust, so we walked behind my dog, a gentle Brittany girl named Ginny. Pheasants were the game, pioneer birds that had colonized territory once belonging to bobwhite. In his day, pheasants were a half-day's journey north. Now, they were the gaudy emissaries of a new age.

The first day brought two fat roosters, both mine. He could scarcely hold a gun, his hands gnarled by a disease named after a surgeon attached to Napoleon's army, a hereditary ailment that appeared in my own right hand just last year. Those eyes, once able to spot a squirrel at a distance where I could scarcely see the tree, had no more depth than a marble left too long in the sun.

Next morning, he uncased his gun, the same old Remington pump, and looked at it for a moment.

"I'm gonna shoot you today," he said, "even if I have to shoot you into the ground."

An hour and three hens later, Ginny made game on a hillside thigh-deep in grass. He was fifty yards away, watching. I'd done everything short of carrying him to keep him close to the dog, but he went his own way, seeming to follow some dog that I couldn't see. Now, I waved him over; he waved me in.

It was a cockbird, colorful as the finest sin. I concentrated on the tip of his tail and shot a barrel's-length behind. The bird scaled south, finally looping into a patch of brush. Ginny gave me a funny look.

This time we walked together, down to where we had him marked. Ginny circled the brush and stopped, taut as a bowstring. I gave him the old, familiar motion that meant "your turn," and he stepped in, gun high and ready.

Cock pheasants, I believe, are the only birds in the world that swear when you make them fly. This one came up like the chimes of doom, in a roar of wings and a crackle of avian invective. The old man lifted his gun in those crippled hands, tracking up the tailfeathers, past the red cheek-patches, swinging beyond the beak into daylight, and watched him fly away.

Back at the car, I poured coffee while he tickled Ginny's ear and coaxed her into the back of the Blazer. A mile of gravel crunched under the tires before he spoke.

"When you go home tomorrow, I want you to take my gun with you."

I looked over to see him staring straight ahead down the road, grinning as if at some private understanding between old friends.

The chapters of this book first appeared, in somewhat different form and often under different titles, in the following magazines:

Sporting Classics: "Coming to Terms," November/December 1993, January/February 1994; "Over-Under or Side-by-Side," January/February 1990; "Who Killed Sweet Sixteen?" July/August 1985; "Twenty-Eight to the Pound," January/February 1987; "Steamwhistles and Screw-Ins," May/June 1987; "Buying Guns at a Distance," July/August 1988; "The Pinfire," September/October 1989; "Safety Systems," January/February 1989; "The Electric Gun," May/June 1988; "A Case History of the Shotshell," November/December 1987; "A Heretic's View of Sporting Clays," November/December 1990; "Women and Shooting," September/October 1987; "Flying Your Guns," September/October 1990; "Nifty Tricks," May/June 1990

Gun Dog: "A Toast to the Trigger," December 1991/January 1992; "More About Triggers," April/May 1992; "Striking a Balance," February/March 1991; "A Fitting End," April/May 1993; "Practical Chokes," February/March 1993; "Buying Smart," October/November 1992; "Eyes," June/July 1991; "Hands," August/September 1991; "Technique," October/November 1991; "When Less is More," October/November 1991, December 1991/January 1992; "A Hard Look at Shot," April/May 1991; "Gunning John Ringneck," August/September 1992; "Knowing How, Knowing When," December 1989/January 1990; "The Second Shot," (l.e.) February/March 1994; "A Checkered Past," (l.e.) June/July 1994

Shooting Sportsman: "Honey and Smoke," August/September 1991; "Wizardry in Walnut," October/November 1991; "The Monstrous Horrendum," January/February 1992

The Double Gun Journal: "True Confessions," Premiere Issue, Winter 1990

Index